ADRP 3-0
UNIFIED LAND OPERATIONS

MAY 2012

DISTRIBUTION RESTRICTION:
Approved for public release; distribution is unlimited.

HEADQUARTERS, DEPARTMENT OF THE ARMY

This publication is available at Army Knowledge Online (https://armypubs.us.army.mil/doctrine/index.html).

Army Doctrine Reference Publication
No. 3-0

Headquarters
Department of the Army
Washington, DC, 16 May 2012

Unified Land Operations

Contents

Page

Figures

Tables

Preface

Army Doctrine Reference Publication (ADRP) 3-0 augments the unified land operations doctrine established in Army Doctrine Publication (ADP) 3-0, *Unified Land Operations*. This manual expands the discussion on the overarching guidance on unified land operations and the Army's core competencies of combined arms maneuver and wide area security. It accounts for the uncertain and ever-changing nature of operations and recognizes that military operations are foremost a human undertaking. It constitutes the Army's view of how to conduct prompt and sustained operations on land and sets the foundation for developing the other principles, tactics, techniques, and procedures detailed in subordinate doctrine publications. Combined with ADP 3-0, the doctrine in ADRP 3-0 provides the foundation for the Army's operational concept of unified land operations. This manual forms the foundation for training and Army education system curricula on unified land operations.

The principal audience for ADRP 3-0 is all members of the profession of arms. Commanders and staffs of Army headquarters serving as joint task force or multinational headquarters should also refer to applicable joint or multinational doctrine concerning the range of military operations and joint or multinational forces. Trainers and educators throughout the Army will also use this manual.

Commanders, staffs, and subordinates ensure their decisions and actions comply with applicable United States, international, and, in some cases, host-nation laws and regulations. Commanders at all levels ensure their Soldiers operate in accordance with the law of war and the rules of engagement. (See Field Manual [FM] 27-10.)

ADRP 3-0 uses joint terms where applicable. Selected joint and Army terms and definitions appear in both the glossary and the text. Terms for which ADRP 3-0 is the proponent publication (the authority) are marked with an asterisk (*) in the glossary. Definitions for which ADRP 3-0 is the proponent publication are boldfaced in the text. These terms and their definitions will be in the next revision of FM 1-02. For other definitions shown in the text, the term is italicized and the number of the proponent publication follows the definition.

ADRP 3-0 applies to the Active Army, Army National Guard (ARNG)/Army National Guard of the United States (ARNGUS), and United States Army Reserve (USAR) unless otherwise stated.

The proponent of ADRP 3-0 is the United States Army Combined Arms Center. The preparing agency is the Combined Arms Doctrine Directorate, United States Army Combined Arms Center. Send comments and recommendations on a DA Form 2028 (Recommended Changes to Publications and Blank Forms) to Commander, United States Army Combined Arms Center, Fort Leavenworth, ATTN: ATZL-MCK-D (ADRP 3-0), 300 McPherson Avenue, Fort Leavenworth, KS 66027-2337; by e-mail to usarmy.leavenworth.mccoe.mbx.cadd-org-mailbox@mail.mil; or submit an electronic DA Form 2028.

Acknowledgments

The copyright owners listed here have granted permission to reproduce material from their works.

On War, by Carl von Clausewitz, edited and translated by Michael Howard and Peter Paret. Reproduced with permission of Princeton University Press. Copyright © 1984.

Introduction

Army Doctrine Reference Publication (ADRP) 3-0, *Unified Land Operations*, is the first ADRP released under Doctrine 2015. ADRP 3-0 expands on the foundations and tenets found in Army Doctrine Publication (ADP) 3-0. This ADRP expands on the doctrine of unified land operations found in ADP 3-0. The publication of ADP 3-0 shifted the Army's operational concept from full spectrum operations to unified land operations.

ADRP 3-0 makes numerous changes from the now obsolete 2011 Field Manual (FM) 3-0, Change 1. The most significant change is the introduction of unified land operations as the Army's operational concept. The doctrine of unified land operations describes how the Army demonstrates its core competencies of combined arm maneuver and wide area security through decisive action. The term *decisive action* replaces the term *full spectrum operations* as the concept of continuous, simultaneous offense, defense, stability, or defense support of civil authorities. *Defense support of civil authorities* replaces *civil support* as a task under decisive action. ADRP 3-0 expands the discussion of the foundations and tenets of unified land operations, as well as the operational framework found in ADP 3-0.

Additional changes in ADRP 3-0 from the now obsolete 2011 FM 3-0, Change 1, includes a discussion of the *range of military operations* replacing the *spectrum of conflict* as well as a discussion of *information collection* replacing *intelligence, reconnaissance, and surveillance* (known as ISR). These changes in ADRP 3-0 now better align Army doctrine with the joint discussion of the principles of joint operations.

ADRP 3-0 remains generally consistent with the now obsolete 2011 FM 3-0, Change 1, on key topics while adopting updated terminology and concepts as necessary. These topics include the discussion of an operational environment and the operational and mission variables, as well as the discussions of unified action, law of land warfare, and combat power. As in the now obsolete 2011, FM 3-0, Change 1, mission command remains both a philosophy of command and a warfighting function. Finally, ADRP 3-0 maintains combined arms as the application of arms that multiplies Army forces' effectiveness in all operations.

ADRP 3-0 contains four chapters:

Chapter 1 shortens the discussion of the operational environment found on the now obsolete 2011 FM 3-0, Change 1, and emphasizes military operations. This chapter provides a framework of variables of an operational environment that shape their nature and affect outcomes. The chapter then discusses unified action and joint operations as well as land operations. Finally, this chapter discusses law of land warfare and combined arms.

Chapter 2 introduces the Army's new operational concept of unified land operations. It discusses how commanders apply landpower as part of unified action to defeat the enemy on land and establish conditions that achieve the joint force commander's end state. Chapter 2 discusses how commanders demonstrate the Army's new core competencies of combined arms maneuver and wide area security conducted through decisive action.

Chapter 3 discusses combat power and the warfighting functions used to generate combat power in support of unified land operations. As in the now obsolete 2011 FM 3-0, Change 1, chapter 3 discusses the eight elements of combat power that include the six warfighting functions with leadership and information. Lastly, it discusses how Army forces achieve combined arms through force tailoring, task organization, and mutual support.

Chapter 4 discusses the elements of operational art and the meaning of operational art to Army forces. It elaborates on commanders and staffs applying the elements of operational art to understand, visualize, and describe how to establish conditions to achieve a desired end state. It discusses how operational art represents a creative approach to dealing with the direction of military forces and expresses an informed vision across the levels of war.

Based on current doctrinal changes, certain terms for which ADRP 3-0 is proponent have been added, rescinded, or modified for purposes of this manual. The glossary contains acronyms and defined terms.

Introductory Table-1. New Army terms

Term	Remarks
close area	New term and definition.
cyber electromagnetic activities	New term and definition.
decisive action	New term and definition.
deep area	New term and definition.
defensive task	Replaces *defensive operations*.
offensive task	Replaces *offensive operations*.
supporting effort	New term and definition.
threat	New term and definition.
unified action partners	New term and definition.

Introductory Table-2. Rescinded Army terms

Term	Remarks
full spectrum operations	Rescinded.
intelligence, surveillance, and reconnaissance	Replaced by *information collection*.
intelligence, surveillance, and reconnaissance integration	Rescinded.
intelligence, surveillance, and reconnaissance synchronization	Rescinded.
operational adaptability	Rescinded.
operational theme	Rescinded.
peacetime military engagement	Rescinded.

Introductory Table-3. Modified Army terms

Term	Remarks
approach	Retained based on common English usage. No longer formally defined.
assessment	Adopts the joint definition.
close combat	Modified the definition.
combat power	Modified the definition.
combined arms	Modified the definition.
commander's intent	Adopts the joint definition.
compel	Retained based on common English usage. No longer formally defined.
decisive operation	Modified the definition.
defensive operations	Retained based on common English usage. No longer formally defined.
depth	Retained based on common English usage. No longer formally defined.
direct approach	Retained based on common English usage. No longer formally defined.
disintegrate	Retained based on common English usage. No longer formally defined.
dislocate	Retained based on common English usage. No longer formally defined.
exterior lines	Modified the definition.
fires warfighting function	Modified the definition.
forward operating base	Retained based on common English usage. No longer formally defined.

Introductory Table-3. Modified Army terms (continued)

Term	Remarks
hybrid threat	Modified the definition.
indirect approach	Retained based on common English usage. No longer formally defined.
inform and influence activities	Modified the definition.
intelligence warfighting function	Modified the definition.
interior lines	Modified the definition.
irregular warfare	Retained based on common English usage. No longer formally defined.
line of effort	Modified the definition.
line of operations	Modified the definition.
main effort	Modified the definition.
mission command warfighting function	Modified the definition.
movement and maneuver warfighting function	Modified the definition.
offensive operations	Retained based on common English usage. No longer formally defined.
operational pause	Retained based on common English usage. No longer formally defined.
persistent conflict	Retained based on common English usage. No longer formally defined.
phase	Modified the definition.
rear area	Retained based on common English usage. No longer formally defined.
shaping operation	Modified the definition.
situational awareness	Retained based on common English usage. No longer formally defined.
support	Adopts the joint definition.
support area	Modified the definition.
supporter	Retained based on common English usage. No longer formally defined.
task-organizing	Modified the definition.
unassigned area	Retained based on common English usage. No longer formally defined.
urban operation	Retained based on common English usage. No longer formally defined.

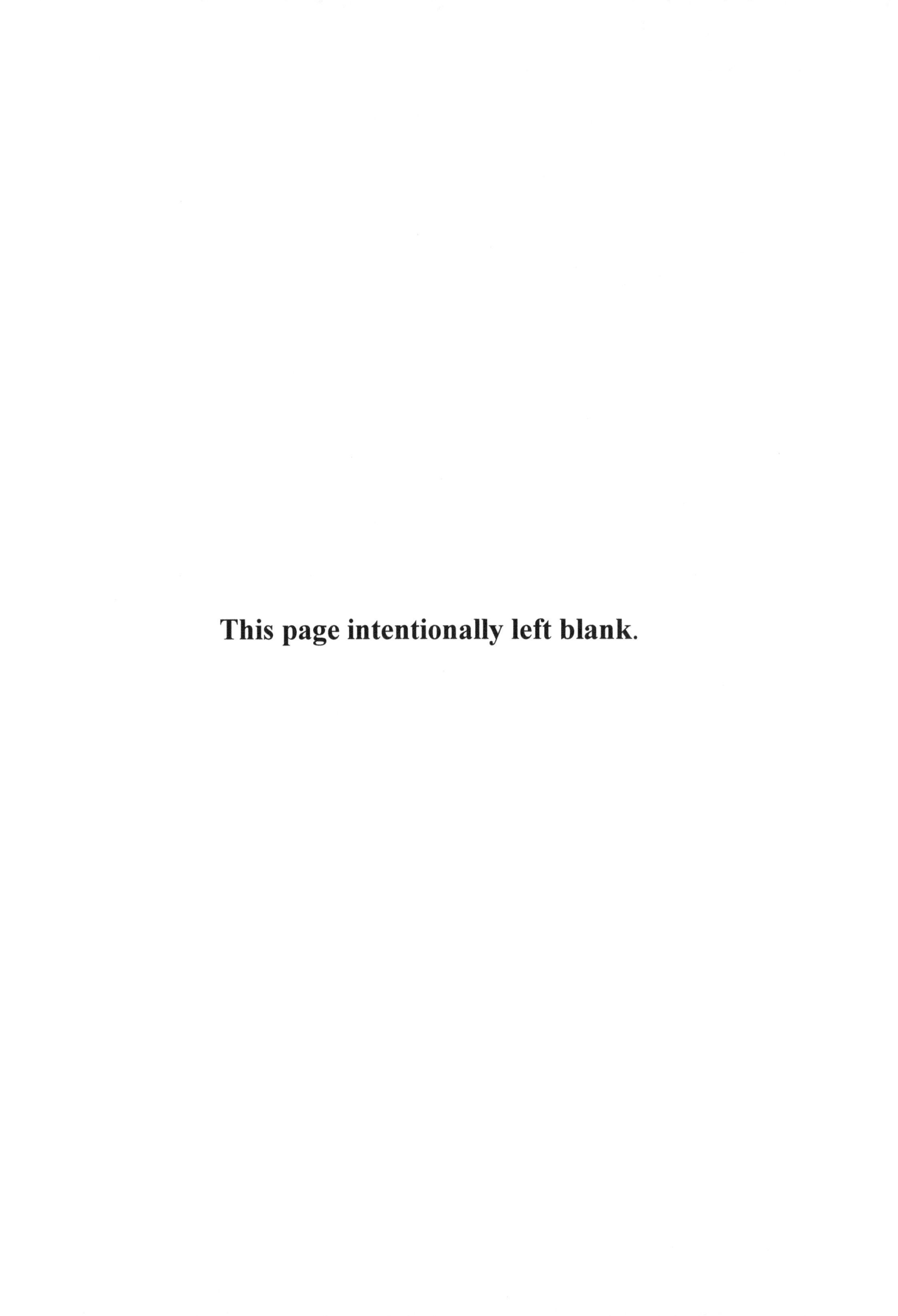

This page intentionally left blank.

Chapter 1

Military Operations

This chapter discusses military operations and their interactions with operational environments and the threats that exist within them. The chapter then discusses unified action and joint operations. Then this chapter discusses land operations. Lastly, the chapter discusses combined arms.

UNIFIED LAND OPERATIONS DEFINED

1-1. *Unified land operations* describes how the Army seizes, retains, and exploits the initiative to gain and maintain a position of relative advantage in sustained land operations through simultaneous offensive, defensive, and stability operations in order to prevent or deter conflict, prevail in war, and create the conditions for favorable conflict resolution (ADP 3-0). Unified land operations is the Army's operational concept and the Army's contribution to unified action.

AN OPERATIONAL ENVIRONMENT

1-2. An *operational environment* is a composite of the conditions, circumstances, and influences that affect the employment of capabilities and bear on the decisions of the commander (JP 3-0). Commanders at all levels have their own operational environments for their particular operations. An operational environment for any specific operation is not just isolated conditions of interacting variables that exist within a specific area of operations. It also involves interconnected influences from the global or regional perspective (for example, politics and economics) that impact on conditions and operations there. Thus, each commander's operational environment is part of a higher commander's operational environment. Likewise, operational environments of commanders at all levels are part of the overall strategic environment, which encompasses general conditions, circumstances, and influences throughout the world that can affect all operations.

1-3. Important trends such as globalization, urbanization, and failed or failing states can affect land operations. These trends can drive instability in an operational environment as well as a continuing state of persistent conflict. Persistent conflict is the protracted confrontation among state, nonstate, and individual actors who are increasingly willing to use violence to achieve their political and ideological ends. In such an operational environment, commanders must seek opportunities for exploiting success. Opportunities may include greater cooperation among the local populace of a town, or perhaps the ability to advance forces along a previously unsecured route. To successfully exploit opportunities, commanders must thoroughly understand and appreciate the changing nature of an operational environment.

1-4. Modern information technology makes cyberspace and the electromagnetic spectrum indispensable for human interaction, including military operations and political competition. These two mediums inherently impact the influence of an operational environment and will be simultaneously congested and contested during operations. All actors—enemy, friendly, or neutral—remain potentially vulnerable to attack by physical means, cyberspace means, electronic means, or a combination thereof. Actions in and through cyberspace and the electromagnetic spectrum can affect the others.

1-5. An operational environment consists of many interrelated variables and subvariables, as well as the relationships and interactions among those variables and subvariables. How the many entities and conditions behave and interact with each other within an operational environment is difficult to discern and always results in differing circumstances. Different actor or audience types do not interpret a single message in the same way. Therefore, no two operational environments are the same.

1-6. In addition, an operational environment continually evolves. This evolution results from humans interacting within an operational environment as well as from their ability to learn and adapt. As people take action in an operational environment, they change that environment. Other variables may also change an operational environment. Some changes are anticipated while others are not. Some changes are immediate and apparent while other changes evolve over time or are extremely difficult to detect.

1-7. The complex and dynamic nature of an operational environment may make determining the relationship between cause and effect difficult and may contribute to the uncertainty of military operations. Commanders must continually assess and reassess their operational environments. They seek a greater understanding of how the changing nature of threats and other variables affect not only their forces but other actors as well. Commanders with their staffs use the Army design methodology, operational variables, and mission variables to analyze an operational environment in support of the operations process.

OPERATIONAL AND MISSION VARIABLES

1-8. An operational environment for each operation differs and evolves as each operation progresses. Army leaders use operational variables to analyze and understand a specific operational environment in which they are conducting operations. They use mission variables to focus on specific elements of an operational environment during mission analysis.

Operational Variables

1-9. Army planners describe conditions of an operational environment in terms of operational variables. Operational variables are those aspects of an operational environment, both military and nonmilitary, that may differ from one operational area to another and affect operations. Operational variables describe not only the military aspects of an operational environment but also the population's influence on it. Army planners analyze an operational environment in terms of eight interrelated operational variables: political, military, economic, social, information, infrastructure, physical environment, and time (PMESII-PT). As soon as a commander and staff have an indication of where their unit will probably deploy, they begin analyzing the operational variables associated with that location. They continue to refine and update that analysis even after receiving a specific mission and throughout the course of the ensuing operation.

Mission Variables

1-10. Upon receipt of a warning order or mission, Army leaders filter relevant information categorized by the operational variables into the categories of the mission variables used during mission analysis. They use the mission variables to refine their understanding of the situation. The mission variables consist of mission, enemy, terrain and weather, troops and support available, time available, and civil considerations (METT-TC). Incorporating the analysis of the operational variables with METT-TC ensures Army leaders consider the best available relevant information about conditions that pertain to the mission.

THREATS

1-11. Threats are a fundamental part of an overall operational environment for any operation but are discussed separately here simply for emphasis. **A *threat* is any combination of actors, entities, or forces that have the capability and intent to harm United States forces, United States national interests, or the homeland**. Threats may include individuals, groups of individuals (organized or not organized), paramilitary or military forces, nation-states, or national alliances. When threats execute their capability to do harm to the United States, they become enemies.

1-12. In general, the various actors in any operational area can qualify as a threat, an enemy, an adversary, a neutral, or a friend. **An *enemy* is a party identified as hostile against which the use of force is authorized**. An enemy is also called a combatant and is treated as such under the law of war. An *adversary* is a party acknowledged as potentially hostile to a friendly party and against which the use of force may be envisaged (JP 3-0). **A *neutral* is a party identified as neither supporting nor opposing friendly or enemy forces**. Land operations often prove complex because a threat, an enemy, an adversary, a neutral, or a friend intermix, often with no easy means to distinguish one from another.

1-13. The term hybrid threat has evolved to capture the seemingly increased complexity of operations, the multiplicity of actors involved, and the blurring between traditional elements of conflict. A *hybrid threat* is **the diverse and dynamic combination of regular forces, irregular forces, terrorist forces, and/or criminal elements unified to achieve mutually benefitting effects**. Hybrid threats combine regular forces governed by international law, military tradition, and custom with unregulated forces that act with no restrictions on violence or their targets. These may involve nation-state actors that employ protracted forms of warfare, possibly using proxy forces to coerce and intimidate, or nonstate actors using operational concepts and high-end capabilities traditionally associated with states. Such varied forces and capabilities enable hybrid threats to capitalize on perceived vulnerabilities, making them particularly effective.

1-14. Enemies may employ sophisticated weapons in specific niches to attack perceived U.S. weaknesses. They may threaten to employ chemical, biological, radiological, or nuclear weapons, targeting concentrations of U.S. forces and urban centers. When projecting power into a region, Army leaders may find themselves without one or more of the advantages they normally have. U.S. forces encountering new and unanticipated enemy capabilities have to rapidly adapt while engaging in operations. Enemies may organize themselves for highly decentralized operations over a protracted period. They will work to secure the active support of other regional powers and supporters. Enemies seek to create disruptive effects oriented toward U.S. activities within the homeland through cyber attacks and terrorism.

1-15. Enemies often choose to fight among the people. Enemies have increasingly attempted to use people and urban settings to their advantage. They seek populations for refuge from, to draw support from, and to shield against attack and detection by U.S. forces. This affects the manner in which Soldiers apply force to achieve success in a conflict.

1-16. For Army forces, the dynamic relationships among friendly forces, enemy forces, and the variables of an operational environment make land operations dynamic and complicated. Regardless of the location or threat, Army forces must synchronize actions to achieve unity of effort that ensures mission accomplishment. They do this as a vital partner in unified action.

UNIFIED ACTION

1-17. *Unified action* is the synchronization, coordination, and/or integration of the activities of governmental and nongovernmental entities with military operations to achieve unity of effort (JP 1). As military forces synchronize actions, they achieve unity of effort. Unified action includes actions of military forces synchronized with activities of other government agencies, nongovernmental and intergovernmental organizations, and the private sector. Military forces play a key role in unified action before, during, and after operations through engagement. The Army's contribution to unified action is unified land operations. (See chapter 2.)

1-18. Army forces coordinate operations with unified action partners. **Unified action partners are those military forces, governmental and nongovernmental organizations, and elements of the private sector with whom Army forces plan, coordinate, synchronize, and integrate during the conduct of operations.** Unified action partners include joint forces and components, multinational forces, and U.S. government agencies and departments.

1-19. Interagency coordination is inherent in unified action. Within the context of Department of Defense involvement, *interagency coordination* is Within the context of Department of Defense involvement, the coordination that occurs between elements of Department of Defense, and engaged US Government agencies and departments for the purpose of achieving an objective (JP 3-0). Army forces conduct and participate in interagency coordination using strategic communication and defense support to public diplomacy.

1-20. Combatant commanders play a pivotal role in unified action. However, subordinate commanders also integrate and synchronize their operations directly with the activities and operations of other military forces and nonmilitary organizations in their areas of operations. Additionally, activities of the host nation and local populace should be considered. For the Army, this is unified land operations.

1-21. Unified action may require interorganizational coordination to build the capacity of our partners. *Interorganizational coordination* is the interaction that occurs among elements of the Department of

Defense; engaged United States Government agencies; state, territorial, local, and tribal agencies; foreign military forces and government agencies; intergovernmental organizations; nongovernmental organizations; and the private sector (JP 3-08). Building partner capacity secures populations, protects infrastructure, and strengthens institutions as a means of protecting common security interests. Building partner capacity is the outcome of comprehensive interorganizational activities, programs, and military-to-military engagements that enhance the ability of partners to establish security, governance, economic development, essential services, rule of law, and other critical government functions. The Army integrates capabilities of the operating and generating forces to support interorganizational capacity-building efforts, primarily through security cooperation interactions.

1-22. *Security cooperation* is all Department of Defense interactions with foreign defense establishments to build defense relationships that promote specific US security interests, develop allied and friendly military capabilities for self-defense and multinational operations, and provide US forces with peacetime and contingency access to a host nation (JP 3-22). Security cooperation provides the means to build partner capacity. The interactions of security cooperation encourage and enable international partners to work with the United States to achieve strategic objectives. These objectives include—

- Building defensive and security relationships that promote specific U.S. security interests, including all international armaments cooperation activities and security assistance activities.
- Developing allied and friendly military capabilities for self-defense and multinational operations.
- Providing U.S. forces with peacetime and contingency access to host nations.

1-23. Supported by appropriate policy, legal frameworks, and authorities, the Army supports the objectives of the combatant commander's campaign plan. The plan supports the objectives by leading security cooperation interactions, specifically those involving security force assistance and foreign internal defense for partner units, institutions, and security sector functions. The operating and generating forces contribute to security sector programs. These programs professionalize and develop secure partner capacity so enabling synchronized and sustained operations. Army security cooperation interactions enable other interorganizational efforts to build partner capacity. Army operating forces—to include special operations forces—advise, train, assist, and equip partner units to develop unit and individual proficiency in security operations. This type of Department of Defense mission is referred to as foreign internal defense. Army generating forces advise and train partner generating forces activities to build institutional capacity for professional education, force generation, and force sustainment.

COOPERATION WITH CIVILIAN ORGANIZATIONS

1-24. Commanders understand the respective roles and capabilities of civilian organizations and contractors in unified action. Other government agencies work with the military and are part of a national chain of command under the President of the United States.

1-25. Civilian organizations—such as other government agencies, intergovernmental organizations, and nongovernmental organizations—bring resources and capabilities that can help establish host-nation civil authority and capabilities. Most civilian organizations are not under military control nor does the American ambassador or a United Nations commissioner control them. Civilian organizations have different organizational cultures and norms. Some may be willing to work with Army forces; others may not. Also, civilian organizations may arrive well after military operations have begun. Thus, personal contact and rapport building are essential. Command emphasis on immediate and continuous coordination encourages effective cooperation. Commanders should establish liaison with civilian organizations to integrate their efforts as much as possible with Army and joint operations. Civil affairs units typically establish this liaison.

1-26. Army forces provide sustainment and security for civilian organizations when directed since many of these organizations lack these capabilities. One example of a civilian organization is an other government agency. Within the context of interagency coordination, an *other government agency* is a non Department of Defense agency of the United States Government (JP 1). Other government agencies include but are not limited to Departments of State, Justice, Transportation, and Agriculture.

1-27. A second example of a civilian organization is an intergovernmental organization. An *intergovernmental organization* is an organization created by a formal agreement between two or more governments on a global, regional, or functional basis to protect and promote national interests shared by member states (JP 3-08). Intergovernmental organizations may be established on a global, regional, or functional basis for wide-ranging or narrowly defined purposes. Examples include the United Nations and European Union.

1-28. Finally, a *nongovernmental organization* is a private, self-governing, not-for-profit organization dedicated to alleviating human suffering; and/or promoting education, health care, economic development, environmental protection, human rights, and conflict resolution; and/or encouraging the establishment of democratic institutions and civil society (JP 3-08). Nongovernmental organizations are independent, diverse, flexible organizations focused on grassroots that range from primary relief and development providers to human rights, civil society, and conflict resolution organizations. Their mission is often one of a humanitarian nature and not one of assisting the military in accomplishing its objectives. Examples include Cooperative for Assistance and Relief Everywhere (known as CARE) and Doctors Without Borders.

1-29. A contractor is a person or business operating under a legal agreement who provides products or services for pay. A contractor furnishes supplies and services or performs work at a certain price or rate based on the contract terms. Contracted support includes traditional goods and services support but may also include interpreter communications, infrastructure, and other related support. Contractor employees include contractors authorized to accompany the force as a formal part of the force and local national employees who normally have no special legal status.

MULTINATIONAL OPERATIONS

1-30. *Multinational operations* is a collective term to describe military actions conducted by forces of two or more nations, usually undertaken within the structure of a coalition or alliance (JP 3-16). While each nation has its own interests, and often participates within limitations of national caveats, all nations bring value to the operation. Each nation's force has unique capabilities, and each usually contributes to the operation's legitimacy in terms of international or local acceptability. (See FM 3-16 on multinational operations.)

1-31. An *alliance* is the relationship that results from a formal agreement between two or more nations for broad, long-term objectives that further the common interests of the members (JP 3-0). Military alliances, such as the North Atlantic Treaty Organization (known as NATO), allow partners to establish formal, standard agreements.

1-32. A *coalition* is an arrangement between two or more nations for common action (JP 5-0). Nations usually form coalitions for focused, short-term purposes. A coalition action is an action outside the bounds of established alliances, usually for single occasions or longer cooperation in a narrow sector of common interest. Army forces may conduct coalition actions under the authority of a United Nations resolution.

1-33. An Army officer assigned to a multinational force faces many demands. These include dealing with cultural issues, different languages, interoperability challenges, national caveats on the use of respective forces, and underdeveloped methods and systems for commanding and controlling. Commanders analyze the mission's peculiar requirements to exploit the multinational force's advantages and compensate for its limitations.

1-34. Multinational sustainment requires detailed planning and coordination. Normally, each nation provides a national support element to sustain its deployed forces. However, integrated multinational sustainment may improve efficiency and effectiveness. When directed, an Army theater sustainment command can provide logistics and other support to multinational forces. Integrating support requirements of several nations' forces, often spread over considerable distances and across international boundaries, is challenging. Commanders consider multinational force capabilities, such as mine clearance, that may exceed U.S. capabilities.

1-35. Unified action requires Army leaders who can understand, influence, and cooperate with leaders from all unified action partners. The Army depends on its joint partners for capabilities that do not reside within the Army; Army forces cannot operate effectively without support from those joint partners. Likewise, government agencies outside the Department of Defense possess knowledge, skills, and capabilities necessary for success. The active cooperation of partners often allows Army leaders to capitalize on organizational strengths while offsetting weaknesses. Only by creating a shared understanding and purpose through collaboration and dialogue with all elements of the friendly force—a key element of mission command—can Army leaders integrate their actions within unified action and synchronize their own efforts and operations. (See Army doctrine on mission command for a detailed discussion of mission command.)

JOINT OPERATIONS

1-36. Services may accomplish tasks and missions in support of Department of Defense (DOD) objectives. However, the DOD primarily employs two or more services in a single operation, particularly in combat, through joint operations. The general term, *joint operations*, describes military actions conducted by joint forces or by Service forces employed under command relationships. A joint force is one composed of significant elements, assigned or attached, of two or more military departments operating under a single joint force commander.

1-37. When conducting operations for a joint force commander, Army forces achieve unified action by synchronizing actions with the activities of components of the joint force and unified action partners. This synchronization occurs across the range of military operations during—

- Military engagement, security cooperation, and deterrence.
- Crisis response and limited contingency operations.
- Major operations and campaigns.

1-38. Military operations vary in purpose, scale, risk, and intensity (see JP 3-0). They include relatively benign, routine, and recurring military operations in peacetime; specific combat and noncombat responses to contingencies and crises as they occur; and less frequent, large-scale combat operations typical of wartime conditions. Army forces are designed, organized, equipped, and trained to accomplish many military operations. Table 1-1 lists examples of military operations. (See JP 1 for a discussion of the range of military operations.)

Table 1-1. Examples of operations and their applicable doctrine

Arms control and disarmament (JP 3-0)	Large-scale combat (FM 3-90)
Civil support (JP 3-28 and FM 3-28)	Noncombatant evacuation (JP 3-68)
Civil-military operations (JP 3-57)	Peace operations (JP 3-07.3)
Combating terrorism (JP 3-07.2)	Raid (FM 3-90)
Combating weapons of mass destruction (JP 3-40)	Recovery operations (JP 3-50 and FM 3-50.1)
Counterinsurgency (JP 3-24 and FM 3-24)	Security force assistance (AR 12-1 and FM 3-07.1)
Enforcement of sanctions (JP 3-0)	Show of force (JP 3-0)
Foreign humanitarian assistance (JP 3-29)	Stability tasks (FM 3-07)
Foreign internal defense (JP 3-22 and FM 3-05.2)	Strike (JP 3-0)
Homeland defense (JP 3-27 and FM 3-28)	Unconventional warfare (JP 3-05 and FM 3-05)

1-39. Joint operations exploit the advantages of interdependent Service capabilities through unified action, and joint planning integrates military power with other instruments of national power to achieve a desired military end state. The end state is the set of required conditions that defines achievement of the commander's objectives. Joint planning connects the strategic end state to the joint force commander's operational campaign design and ultimately to tactical missions. Joint force commanders use campaigns and major joint operations to translate their operational-level actions into strategic results. Planning for a campaign is appropriate when the contemplated military operations exceed the scope of a single major operation. Campaigns are always joint operations. (See chapter 2 for a discussion of campaigns.)

LAND OPERATIONS

1-40. The Army's primary mission is to organize, train, and equip forces to conduct prompt and sustained land combat operations and perform such other duties, not otherwise assigned by law, as may be prescribed by the President or the Secretary of Defense. The Army does this through its operational concept of unified land operations. Army doctrine aligns with joint doctrine and takes into account the nature of land operations. The command and control of operations on land fundamentally differs from other types of military operations.

1-41. The dynamic relationships among friendly forces, enemy forces, and the other variables of an operational environment (PMESII-PT and METT-TC) make land operations exceedingly difficult to understand and visualize. Understanding each of these parts separately is important but not sufficient to understand the relationships among them. Friendly forces compete with enemy forces to attain operational advantages within an operational environment. These advantages facilitate Army forces closing with and destroying the enemy with minimal losses to friendly forces as well as civilians and their property.

1-42. Joint doctrine discusses traditional war as a confrontation between nation-states or coalitions of nation-states. This confrontation typically involves small-scale to large-scale, force-on-force military operations in which enemies use various conventional military capabilities against each other. Landpower normally solidifies the outcome, even when it is not the definitive instrument. ***Landpower* is the ability— by threat, force, or occupation—to gain, sustain, and exploit control over land, resources, and people.** Landpower is at the very heart of unified land operations. Landpower includes the ability to—

- Impose the Nation's will on an enemy, by force if necessary.
- Engage to influence, shape, prevent, and deter in an operational environment.
- Establish and maintain a stable environment that sets the conditions for political and economic development.
- Address the consequences of catastrophic events—both natural and man-made—to restore infrastructure and reestablish basic civil services.
- Support and provide a base from which joint forces can influence and dominate the air and maritime domains of an operational environment.

ARMY FORCES—EXPEDITIONARY CAPABILITY AND CAMPAIGN QUALITY

1-43. Future conflicts will place a premium on promptly deploying landpower and constantly adapting to each campaign's unique circumstances as they occur and change. But swift campaigns, however desirable, are the exception. Whenever objectives involve controlling populations or dominating terrain, campaign success usually requires employing landpower for protracted periods. Therefore, the Army combines expeditionary capability and campaign quality to contribute crucial, sustained landpower to unified action.

1-44. Expeditionary capability is the ability to promptly deploy combined arms forces worldwide into any area of operations and conduct operations upon arrival. Expeditionary operations require the ability to deploy quickly with little notice, rapidly shape conditions in the operational area, and operate immediately on arrival exploiting success and consolidating tactical and operational gains. Expeditionary capabilities are more than physical attributes; they begin with a mindset that pervades the force.

1-45. Expeditionary capabilities assure friends, multinational partners, enemies, and adversaries that the Nation is able and willing to deploy the right combination of Army forces to the right place at the right time. Forward deployed units, forward positioned capabilities, and force projection—from anywhere in the world—all contribute to the Army's expeditionary capabilities. Providing joint force commanders with expeditionary capability requires forces organized and equipped to be modular, versatile, and rapidly deployable as well as able to conduct operations with institutions capable of supporting them.

1-46. Campaign quality is the ability to sustain operations as long as necessary and to conclude operations successfully. Army forces are organized, trained, and equipped for endurance. The Army's campaign quality extends its expeditionary capability well beyond deploying combined arms forces that are effective upon arrival. It is an ability to conduct sustained operations for as long as necessary, adapting to unpredictable and often profound changes in an operational environment as the campaign unfolds. Army engagement activities extend expeditionary capability and campaign quality to precombat and postcombat campaign periods.

CLOSE COMBAT

1-47. *Close combat* **is warfare carried out on land in a direct-fire fight, supported by direct and indirect fires and other assets**. Close combat is indispensable and unique to land operations. Only on land do combatants routinely and in large numbers come face-to-face with one another. It underlies most Army efforts in peace and war. When other means fail to drive enemy forces from their positions, Army forces close with and destroy or capture them. The outcome of battles and engagements depends on the Army forces' ability to prevail in close combat.

1-48. Regardless of the importance of technological capabilities, success in the Army's core competencies requires Soldiers to accomplish the mission. Today's operational environment requires Soldiers whose character and competence represent the foundation of a values-based, trained, and ready Army. Today's Soldiers are adaptive and learning while training to perform tasks while alone or in groups. Soldiers and leaders develop the ability to exercise mature judgment and initiative under stress. The Army requires adaptive leaders able to execute the Army's core competencies in an era of persistent conflict. (See Army doctrine on leadership.) Army leaders must remain—

- Competent in their core proficiencies.
- Trained to operate across the range of military operations.
- Able to operate in combined arms teams within unified action and leverage other capabilities in achieving their objectives.
- Culturally astute.
- Courageous enough to use initiative to seek and exploit potential opportunities in a dynamic operational environment.
- Grounded in the Army Values and the Warrior Ethos.
- Opportunistic and offensively minded.

OPERATIONS STRUCTURE

1-49. The operations structure—the operations process, warfighting functions, and operational framework—is the Army's common construct for operations. It allows Army leaders to rapidly and effectively organize effort in a manner commonly understood across the Army. The operations process provides a broadly defined approach to developing and executing operations. The warfighting functions provide an intellectual organization for common critical functions (see chapter 3). The operational framework provides Army leaders with basic conceptual options for visualizing and describing operations.

Operations Process

1-50. The operations process consists of the major mission command activities performed during operations: planning, preparing, executing, and continuously assessing the operation (see Army doctrine on the operations process). The operations process is a commander-led activity, informed by the mission command approach to planning, preparing, executing, and assessing military operations. These activities may be sequential or simultaneous. In fact, they are rarely discrete and often involve a great deal of overlap. Commanders use the operations process to drive the planning necessary to understand, visualize, and describe their unique operational environments; make and articulate decisions; and direct, lead, and assess military operations.

1-51. Planning is the art and science of understanding a situation, envisioning desired future conditions, and laying out effective ways of bringing that future about. Planning consists of two separate but interrelated components: a conceptual component and a detailed component. Successful planning requires the integration of both these components. Army leaders employ three methodologies for planning: the Army design methodology, the military decisionmaking process, and troop leading procedures (see paragraphs 1-53 through 1-55). Commanders determine how much of each methodology to use based on the scope of the problem, their familiarity with it, and the time available.

1-52. Preparation consists of activities that units perform to improve their ability to execute an operation. Execution puts a plan into action by applying combat power to accomplish the mission and using situational understanding to assess progress and make execution and adjustment decisions. Finally, *assessment* is determination of the progress toward accomplishing a task, creating a condition, or achieving an objective (JP 3-0).

The Army Design Methodology

1-53. The Army design methodology is a methodology for applying critical and creative thinking to understand, visualize, and describe unfamiliar problems and approaches to solving them. The Army design methodology is particularly useful as an aid to conceptual thinking about unfamiliar problems. To produce executable plans, commanders integrate it with the detailed planning typically associated with the military decisionmaking process. Commanders who use the Army design methodology may gain a greater understanding of their operational environments and the problems and visualize an appropriate operational approach. With this greater understanding, commanders can provide a clear commander's intent and concept of operations—both required by mission command. Such clarity enables subordinate units and commanders to take initiative. The Army design methodology is iterative and collaborative. As the operations process unfolds, the commander, staff, subordinates, and other partners continue to learn and collaborate to improve their shared understanding. An improved understanding may lead to modifications to their operational approach or an entirely new approach altogether.

The Military Decisionmaking Process

1-54. The military decisionmaking process is also an iterative planning methodology. It integrates activities of the commander, staff, subordinate headquarters, and other partners. This integration enables them to understand the situation and mission; develop, analyze, and compare courses of action; decide on a course of action that best accomplishes the mission; and produce an operation order for execution. The military decisionmaking process applies both conceptual and detailed approaches to thinking but is most closely associated with detailed planning. For unfamiliar problems, executable solutions typically require integrating the Army design methodology with the military decisionmaking process. The military decisionmaking process helps leaders apply thoroughness, clarity, sound judgment, logic, and professional knowledge so they understand situations, develop options to solve problems, and reach decisions. This process helps commanders, staffs, and others think critically and creatively while planning.

Troop Leading Procedures

1-55. Troop leading procedures are a dynamic process used by small-unit leaders to analyze a mission, develop a plan, and prepare for an operation. Heavily weighted in favor of familiar problems and short time frames, organizations with staffs typically do not employ troop leading procedures. More often, leaders use troop leading procedures to solve tactical problems when working alone or with a small group. For example, a company commander may use the executive officer, first sergeant, fire support officer, supply sergeant, and communications sergeant to assist during troop leading procedures.

THE WARFIGHTING FUNCTIONS

1-56. To execute operations, commanders conceptualize capabilities in terms of combat power. Combat power has eight elements: leadership, information, mission command, movement and maneuver, intelligence, fires, sustainment, and protection. The Army collectively describes the last six elements as the warfighting functions. Commanders apply combat power through the warfighting functions using leadership and information. (See chapter 3.)

OPERATIONAL FRAMEWORK

1-57. Army leaders are responsible for clearly articulating their visualization of operations in time, space, purpose, and resources. An established operational framework and associated vocabulary can assist greatly in this task. Army leaders are not bound by any specific framework for conceptually organizing operations, but three operational frameworks have proven valuable in the past. The higher headquarters will direct the specific framework or frameworks to be used by subordinate headquarters; the frameworks should be consistent throughout all echelons.

Deep–Close–Security

1-58. The deep-close-security operational framework has historically been associated with terrain orientation but can be applied to temporal and organizational orientations as well. (See figure 1-1.)

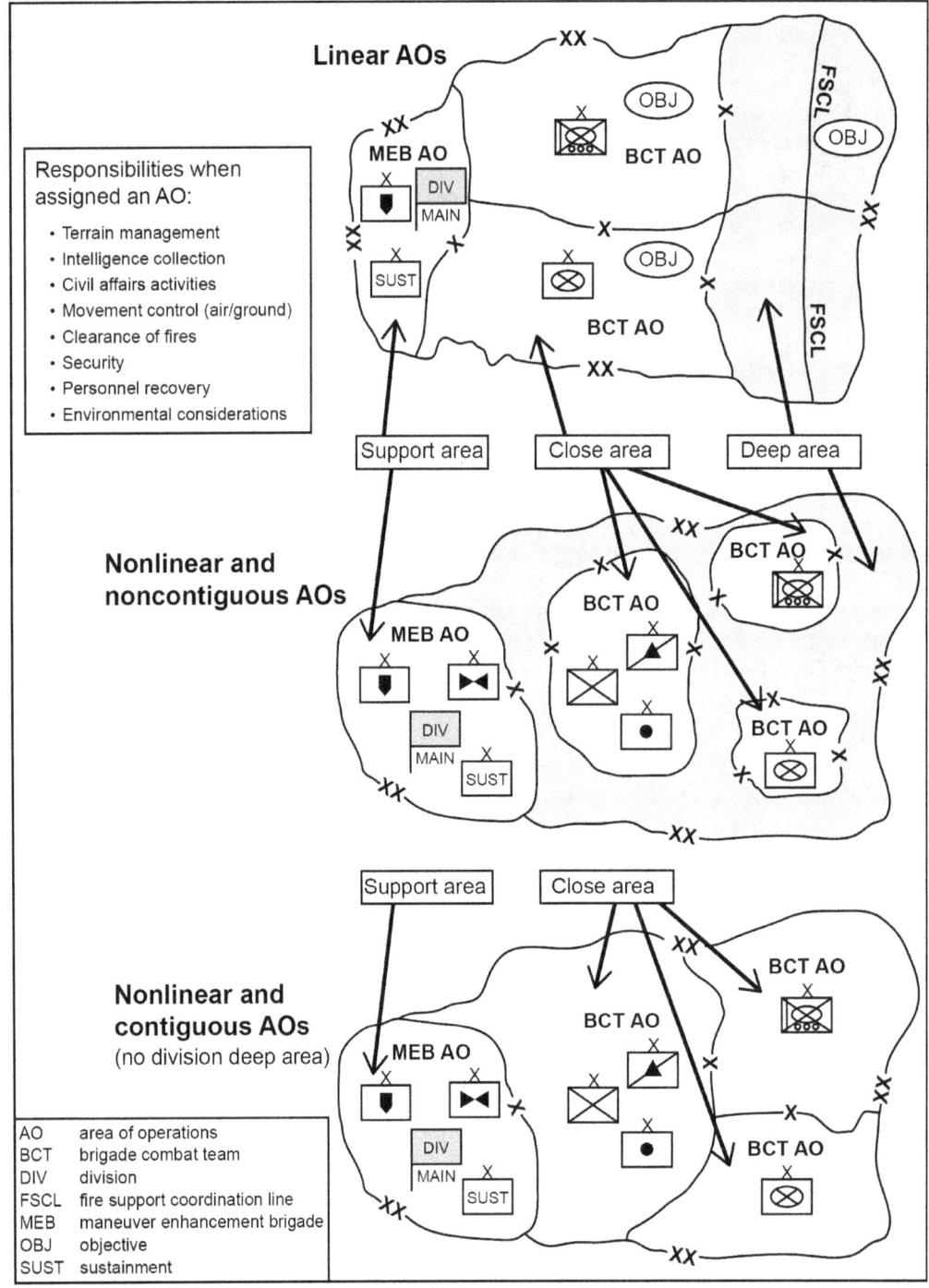

Figure 1-1. Example of deep-close-security operational framework

1-59. Deep operations involve efforts to prevent uncommitted enemy forces from being committed in a coherent manner. The purpose of deep operations is frequently tied to other events distant in time, space or both. Deep operations might aim to disrupt the movement of operational reserves, for example, or prevent the enemy from employing long-range cannon, rocket, or missile fires. In an operational environment where the enemy recruits insurgents from within a population, deep operations might focus on interfering with the recruiting process, disrupting the training of recruits, or eliminating the underlying factors that enable the enemy to recruit.

1-60. In deep operations, a commander may refer to a deep area. **In contiguous areas of operations, a _deep area_ is an area forward of the close area that a commander uses to shape enemy forces before they are encountered or engaged in the close area**. Typically, the deep area extends from the forward boundary of subordinate units to the forward boundary of the controlling echelon in contiguous areas of operations. In this sense, the deep area relates not only in terms of geography but also in terms of purpose and time.

1-61. In noncontiguous areas of operations, the deep area is the area between noncontiguous areas of operations or beyond contiguous areas of operations. The higher headquarters controls deep areas within its area of operations. In some instances, a deep area may focus along a single line of operations. In other instances, a deep area may focus along multiple lines of operations in various directions and distances. The mission variables of METT-TC will impact how leaders define a deep area.

1-62. Close operations are operations that are within a subordinate commander's area of operations. Operations projected in close areas are usually against hostile forces in immediate contact and are often the decisive operation. A close operation requires speed and mobility to rapidly concentrate overwhelming combat power at the critical time and place and to exploit success.

1-63. In close operations, a commander may refer to a close area. **In contiguous areas of operations, a _close area_ is an area assigned to a maneuver force that extends from its subordinates' rear boundaries to its own forward boundary**. Commanders plan to conduct decisive operations through maneuver and fires in the close area and position most of the maneuver force within it. Within the close area, depending on echelon, one unit may conduct the decisive operation while others conduct shaping operations.

1-64. In noncontiguous areas of operations, the close area is the area within the subordinate commanders' areas of operations. The higher commander may redefine the boundaries of specific areas of operations as necessary to shape operations, reallocating resources to ensure subordinate headquarters can adequately cover their assigned areas of operations.

1-65. Security operations involve efforts to provide an early and accurate warning of enemy operations and to provide time and maneuver space within which to react to the enemy. These operations protect the force from surprise and develop the situation to allow the commander to use the force effectively. Security operations include necessary actions to retain freedom of action and ensure uninterrupted support or sustainment of all other operations.

1-66. When associated with a terrain orientation, a commander may conduct area security operations. Area security operations may be offensive or defensive in nature. These operations focus on the protected force, installation, route, or area. Protected forces range from echelon headquarters through artillery and echelon reserves to the sustaining forces. Protected installations can be part of the sustaining base or part of the area's infrastructure. Protected routes and areas involve securing a range from specific points (bridges and defiles) and terrain features (ridgelines and hills) to large population centers and their adjacent areas.

1-67. Operations in noncontiguous areas of operations require commanders to emphasize area security. During offensive and retrograde operations, the speed at which the main body moves provides some measure of security. Rapidly moving units in open terrain can rely on technical assets to provide advance warning of enemy forces. In restrictive terrain, security forces focus on key terrain such as potential choke points.

1-68. In deep, close, and security operations, a commander may refer to a support area. **In contiguous areas of operations, a _support area_ is an area for any command that extends from its rear boundary**

forward to the rear boundary of the next lower level of command. This unit primarily provides a support area as a place to support functions. It is where most of the echelon's sustaining operations occur.

1-69. In noncontiguous areas of operations, the support area is that area defined within the higher commander's area of operations providing a location to base sustainment assets and provide sustainment to the force. The higher headquarters secures the support area if the support area falls outside a subordinate commander's area of operations.

Decisive–Shaping–Sustaining

1-70. The decisive-shaping-sustaining framework lends itself to a broad conceptual orientation. **The *decisive operation* is the operation that directly accomplishes the mission**. It determines the outcome of a major operation, battle, or engagement. The decisive operation is the focal point around which commanders design an entire operation. Multiple subordinate units may be engaged in the same decisive operation. Decisive operations lead directly to the accomplishment of a commander's intent. Commanders typically identify a single decisive operation, but more than one subordinate unit may play a role in a decisive operation.

1-71. **A *shaping operation* is an operation that establishes conditions for the decisive operation through effects on the enemy, other actors, and the terrain**. Inform and influence activities, for example, may integrate Soldier and leader engagement tasks into the operation to reduce tensions between Army units and different ethnic groups through direct contact between Army leaders and local leaders. In combat, synchronizing the effects of rotary- and fixed-wing aircraft, artillery fires, and obscurants to delay or disrupt repositioning forces illustrates shaping operations. Shaping operations may occur throughout the operational area and involve any combination of forces and capabilities. Shaping operations preserve conditions for the success of the decisive operation. Commanders may designate more than one shaping operation.

1-72. **A *sustaining operation* is an operation at any echelon that enables the decisive operation or shaping operation by generating and maintaining combat power**. Sustaining operations differ from decisive and shaping operations in that they focus internally (on friendly forces) rather than externally (on the enemy or environment). They typically address important sustainment and protection actions essential to the success of decisive and shaping operations. Sustaining operations include personnel and logistics support, rear area security, movement control, terrain management, and infrastructure development.

1-73. While sustaining operations are inseparable from decisive and shaping operations, they are not usually decisive themselves. Sustaining operations occur throughout the area of operations, not just within a support area. Failure to sustain normally results in mission failure. Sustaining operations determine how fast Army forces reconstitute and how far Army forces can exploit success.

Main and Supporting Efforts

1-74. The main and supporting efforts operational framework—simpler than other organizing frameworks—focuses on prioritizing effort among subordinate units. Therefore, leaders can use the main and supporting efforts with either the deep-close-security framework or the decisive-shaping-sustaining framework.

1-75. **The *main effort* is a designated subordinate unit whose mission at a given point in time is most critical to overall mission success**. It is usually weighted with the preponderance of combat power. Typically, commanders shift the main effort one or more times during execution. Designating a main effort temporarily prioritizes resource allocation. When commanders designate a unit as the main effort, it receives priority of support and resources. Commanders shift resources and priorities to the main effort as circumstances and the commander's intent require. Commanders may designate a unit conducting a shaping operation as the main effort until the decisive operation commences. However, the unit with primary responsibility for the decisive operation becomes the main effort upon the execution of the decisive operation.

1-76. **A *supporting effort* is a designated subordinate unit with a mission that supports the success of the main effort**. Commanders may provide augmentation to the main effort or develop a supporting plan synchronized with the higher plan. They resource supporting efforts with the minimum assets necessary to accomplish the mission. Forces often realize success of the main effort through success of supporting efforts.

Area of Operations

1-77. When establishing the operational framework, commanders use control measures to assign responsibilities, coordinate fires and maneuver, and control combat operations. One of the most important control measures is the area of operations. An *area of operations* is an operational area defined by the joint force commander for land and maritime forces that should be large enough to accomplish their missions and protect their forces (JP 3-0). For land operations, an area of operations includes subordinate areas of operations as well. The Army command or joint force land component commander is the supported commander within an area of operations designated by the joint force commander for land operations. Within their areas of operations, commanders integrate and synchronize combat power. To facilitate this integration and synchronization, commanders have the authority to designate targeting priority, effects, timing, and effects of fires within their areas of operations.

1-78. Commanders consider a unit's area of influence when assigning it an area of operations. An *area of influence* is a geographical area wherein a commander is directly capable of influencing operations by maneuver or fire support systems normally under the commander's command or control (JP 3-0). The area of influence normally surrounds and includes the area of operations. Understanding the area of influence helps the commander and staff plan branches to the current operation in which the force uses capabilities outside the area of operations. An area of operations should not be substantially larger than the unit's area of influence. Ideally, the area of influence would encompass the entire area of operations. An area of operations that is too large for a unit to control can allow sanctuaries for enemy forces and may limit joint flexibility.

1-79. An *area of interest* is that area of concern to the commander, including the area of influence, areas adjacent thereto, and extending into enemy territory. This area also includes areas occupied by enemy forces who could jeopardize the accomplishment of the mission (JP 3-0). An area of interest for stability or defense support of civil authorities tasks may be much larger than that area associated with the offense and defense.

THE LAW OF WAR AND RULES OF ENGAGEMENT

1-80. Commanders at all levels ensure their Soldiers operate in accordance with the law of war. The law of war—also called the law of armed conflict—is that body of international law, founded upon both treaties and custom, that regulates the conduct of armed hostilities (see FM 27-10). Compliance with the law of war is not situationally dependent, contingent on the nature of the conflict, contingent on the nature of the enemy, nor otherwise optional. All personnel, commanders and Soldiers alike, have an affirmative duty to comply with the law of war at all times. It is therefore incumbent on commanders and leaders at all levels to ensure personnel receive regular and rigorous training on the law of war.

1-81. The law of war's evolution was largely humanitarian in nature and designed to reduce the evils of war. The humanitarian purposes of the law of war are to—

● Protect both combatants and noncombatants from unnecessary suffering.
● Safeguard the rights of persons (those who become prisoners of war, the wounded and sick, and civilians).
● Make the transition to peace easier.

1-82. Functional purposes of the law of war include—

● Preventing the deterioration of good order and discipline within a unit.
● Maintaining and preserving the humanity of the Soldiers involved in a conflict.
● Maintaining the public's support.

1-83. Soldiers consider three important principles that govern the law of war when planning and executing operations: military necessity, distinction, and proportionality. Military necessity requires combat forces to engage in only those acts necessary to accomplish a legitimate military objective. Military objectives are those objects which—by their nature, location, purpose, or use—effectively contribute to military action and whose total or partial destruction, capture, or neutralization, in the circumstances ruling at the time, offers a definite military advantage. Distinction means discriminating between lawful combatant targets and noncombatant targets. The latter may include civilians, civilian property, prisoners of war, and wounded personnel who are out of combat. Proportionality states the anticipated loss of life and damage to property incidental to attacks must not be excessive in relation to the concrete and direct military advantage expected to be gained.

1-84. *Rules of engagement* are directives issued by competent military authority that delineate the circumstances and limitations under which United States forces will initiate and/or continue combat engagement with other forces encountered (JP 1-04). Rules of engagement always recognize the inherent right of self-defense. These rules vary between operations and may change during an operation. Adherence to them ensures Soldiers act consistently with international law, national policy, and military regulations.

1-85. Soldiers deployed to a combat zone overseas follow rules of engagement established by the Secretary of Defense and adjusted for theater conditions by the joint force commander. Within the United States and its territories, Soldiers adhere to rules for the use of force. *Rules for the use of force* consist of directives issued to guide United States forces on the use of force during various operations. These directives may take the form of execute orders, deployment orders, memoranda of agreement, or plans (JP 3-28). There are many similarities between them, for example in the inherent right of self-defense, but they differ in intent. Rules of engagement are by nature permissive measures intended to allow the maximum use of destructive combat power appropriate for the mission. Rules for the use of force are restrictive measures intended to allow only the minimum force necessary to accomplish the mission. The underlying principle is a "continuum of force," a carefully graduated level of response determined by civilians' behavior.

1-86. Soldiers use discipline when applying lethal and nonlethal actions, a necessity for successful operations. Today's threats challenge the morals and ethics of Soldiers. Often an enemy feels no compulsion to respect international laws or conventions and commits atrocities simply to provoke retaliation in kind. The enemy and adversary forces, as well as neutral and friendly forces, take any loss of discipline on the part of Soldiers, distort and exploit it in propaganda, and magnify it through the media. It is therefore crucial that all personnel operate consistently at all times with applicable U.S., international, and in some case host-nation laws and regulation. The challenge to ensure Soldiers remain within legal, moral, and ethical boundaries at all times rests heavily on small-unit and company-grade leaders charged with maintaining good order and discipline within their respective units. The Soldier's Rules in Army Regulation (AR) 350-1 distill the essence of the law of war. They outline the ethical and lawful conduct required of Soldiers in operations. (Table 1-2 lists the Soldier's Rules.)

Table 1-2. The Soldier's Rules

• Soldiers fight only enemy combatants.
• Soldiers do not harm enemies who surrender. They disarm them and turn them over to their superior.
• Soldiers do not kill or torture any personnel in their custody.
• Soldiers collect and care for the wounded, whether friend or foe.
• Soldiers do not attack medical personnel, facilities, or equipment.
• Soldiers destroy no more than the mission requires.
• Soldiers treat civilians humanely.
• Soldiers do not steal. Soldiers respect private property and possessions.
• Soldiers should do their best to prevent violations of the law of war.
• Soldiers report all violations of the law of war to their superior.

COMBINED ARMS

1-87. Applying combat power depends on combined arms to achieve its full destructive, disruptive, informational, and constructive potential. **Combined arms is the synchronized and simultaneous application of arms to achieve an effect greater than if each arm was used separately or sequentially.** Combined arms integrates leadership, information, and each of the warfighting functions and their supporting systems. Used destructively, combined arms integrates different capabilities so that counteracting one makes the enemy vulnerable to another. Used constructively, combined arms multiplies the effectiveness and efficiency of Army capabilities used in stability or defense support of civil authorities.

1-88. Combined arms uses the capabilities of each warfighting function and information in complementary and reinforcing capabilities. Complementary capabilities protect the weaknesses of one system or organization with the capabilities of a different warfighting function. For example, commanders use artillery (fires) to suppress an enemy bunker complex pinning down an infantry unit (movement and maneuver). The infantry unit then closes with and destroys the enemy. In this example, the fires warfighting function complements the movement and maneuver warfighting function.

1-89. Reinforcing capabilities combine similar systems or capabilities within the same warfighting function to increase the function's overall capabilities. In urban operations, for example, infantry, aviation, and armor (movement and maneuver) often operate close to each other. This combination reinforces the protection, maneuver, and direct fire capabilities of each. The infantry protects tanks from enemy infantry and antitank systems; tanks provide protection and firepower for the infantry. Attack helicopters maneuver above buildings to fire from positions of advantage, while other aircraft help sustain the ground elements. Army space-enabled capabilities and services such as communications and global positioning satellites enable communications, navigation, situational awareness, protection, and sustainment of land forces.

1-90. Joint capabilities—such as close air support and special operations forces—can complement or reinforce Army capabilities throughout both the generating force and the operating force. The generating force consists of those Army organizations whose primary mission is to generate and sustain the operational Army's capabilities for employment by joint force commanders. Operating forces consist of those forces whose primary missions are to participate in combat and the integral supporting elements thereof. Often, commanders in the operating force and commanders in the generating force subdivide specific responsibilities. Army generating force capabilities and organizations are linked to operating forces through co-location and reachback.

1-91. Combined arms multiplies Army forces' effectiveness in all operations. Units operating without support of other capabilities generate less combat power and may not accomplish their mission. Employing combined arms requires highly trained Soldiers, skilled leadership, effective staff work, and integrated information systems. Commanders synchronize combined arms through mission command to apply the effects of combat power to the best advantage. They conduct simultaneous combinations of offensive, defensive, and stability or defense support of civil authorities tasks to defeat an opponent on land and establish conditions that achieve the joint force commander's end state.

This page intentionally left blank.

Chapter 2

The Army's Operational Concept

This chapter discusses the Army's operational concept in detail. It first discusses the concept of unified land operations. Then it discusses the foundations of unified land operations. Lastly, this chapter discusses the tenets of unified land operations.

GOAL OF UNIFIED LAND OPERATIONS

2-1. The goal of unified land operations is to apply landpower as part of unified action to defeat the enemy on land and establish conditions that achieve the joint force commander's end state. Today's operational environments require commanders to demonstrate the core competencies of combined arms maneuver and wide area security conducted through offensive, defensive, and stability or defense support of civil authorities tasks to reach this goal.

2-2. Unified land operations is the Army's operational concept and the Army's contribution to unified action. The central idea of unified land operations is how the Army seizes, retains, and exploits the initiative to gain and maintain a position of relative advantage in sustained land operations through simultaneous offensive, defensive, and stability or defense support of civil authorities tasks to prevent or deter conflict, prevail in war, and create the conditions for favorable conflict resolution. Where possible, military forces working with unified action partners seek to prevent or deter threats. However, if necessary, military forces possess the capability in unified land operations to prevail over aggression.

FOUNDATIONS OF UNIFIED LAND OPERATIONS

2-3. By integrating the four foundations of unified land operations—initiative, decisive action, Army core competencies, and mission command—Army commanders can achieve strategic success. Strategic success requires full integration of U.S. military operations with the efforts of unified action partners. The foundations of unified land operations begin and end with the exercise of individual and operational initiative. Initiative is used to gain a position of advantage that degrades and defeats the enemy throughout the depth of an organization. The Army demonstrates its core competencies through decisive action. The Army's two core competencies—combined arms maneuver and wide area security—provide the means for balancing the application of Army warfighting functions within the tactical actions and tasks inherent in the offense, defense, and stability overseas, or defense support of civil authorities in the United States. By demonstrating the two core competencies, Army forces defeat or destroy an enemy, seize or occupy key terrain, protect or secure critical assets and populations, and prevent the enemy from gaining a position of advantage. The philosophy of mission command—the exercise of authority and direction by the commander using mission orders to enable disciplined initiative within the commander's intent—guides leaders in the execution of unified land operations (see Army doctrine on mission command).

INITIATIVE

2-4. All Army operations aim to seize, retain, and exploit the initiative and achieve decisive results. *Operational initiative* **is setting or dictating the terms of action throughout an operation.** *Individual initiative* **is the willingness to act in the absence of orders, when existing orders no longer fit the situation, or when unforeseen opportunities or threats arise.** Initiative gives all operations the spirit, if not the form, of the offense. It originates in the principle of war of the offensive. This principle goes beyond simply attacking. It requires action to change the situation on the ground. Risk and opportunity are intrinsic in seizing the initiative. To seize the initiative, commanders evaluate and take prudent risks as necessary to exploit opportunities. Initiative requires constant effort to control tempo and momentum while maintaining freedom of action. This offensive mindset, with its focus on initiative, is central to the Army's operational concept and guides all leaders in the performance of their duty. It emphasizes opportunity created by developing the situation through decisive action, whether in offensive, defensive, stability, or defense support of civil authorities tasks.

2-5.   In combined arms maneuver, commanders compel the enemy to respond to friendly action. In the offense, it involves taking the fight to the enemy and never allowing enemy forces to recover from the initial shock of the attack. In the defense, it involves preventing the enemy from achieving success and then counterattacking to seize the initiative. The object is more than just killing enemy personnel and destroying their equipment. Combined arms maneuver forces the enemy to react continuously and finally to be driven into untenable positions. Seizing the initiative pressures enemy commanders into abandoning their preferred courses of action, accepting too much risk, or making costly mistakes. As enemy mistakes occur, friendly forces seize opportunities and create new avenues for exploitation. Ultimately, combined arms maneuver aims to break the enemy's will through relentless and continuous pressure.

2-6.   Wide area security is about retaining the initiative by improving civil conditions and applying combat power to prevent the situation from deteriorating. It is also about preventing the enemy from regaining the initiative—retaining the initiative in the face of enemy attempts to regain it for themselves. Commanders identify nonmilitary but critical objectives to achieving the end state. Such objectives may include efforts to ensure effective governance, reconstruction projects that promote social well-being, and consistent actions to improve public safety. All these objectives contribute to retaining the initiative in wide area security.

2-7.   Army forces retain the initiative. An enemy insurgent cannot allow stability tasks to succeed without serious consequences and must react. As the enemy reacts, Army forces retain the initiative by modifying their own lethal and nonlethal actions, forcing the enemy to change plans and remain on the defensive. Army forces retain the initiative by anticipating both enemy actions and civil requirements and by acting positively to address them. While performing defense support of civil authorities tasks, Soldiers work closely with their civilian counterparts to remedy the conditions threatening lives, property, and domestic order. In some situations, rapid and determined action by Army forces becomes the stimulus that prompts a demoralized civilian community to begin recovery.

2-8.   Seizing, retaining, and exploiting the initiative depends on individual initiative. Military history contains many instances where a subordinate's action or inaction significantly affected the tactical, operational, or even strategic situation. When opportunity occurs, it is often fleeting. Subordinate leaders need to act quickly, even as they report the situation to their commanders. Individual initiative is a key component of mission command; as subordinate commanders exercise individual initiative, higher commanders give them the authority to do so.

DECISIVE ACTION

2-9.   Army forces demonstrate the Army's core competencies through *decisive action*—**the continuous, simultaneous combinations of offensive, defensive, and stability or defense support of civil authorities tasks**. In unified land operations, commanders seek to seize, retain, and exploit the initiative while synchronizing their actions to achieve the best effects possible. Operations conducted outside the United States and its territories simultaneously combine three elements—offense, defense, and stability. Within the United States and its territories, decisive action combines the elements of defense support of civil authorities and, as required, offense and defense to support homeland defense. (See figure 2-1.)

2-10. Decisive action begins with the commander's intent and concept of operations. As a single, unifying idea, decisive action provides direction for the entire operation. Based on a specific idea of how to accomplish the mission, commanders and staffs refine the concept of operations during planning. They adjust it throughout the operation as subordinates develop the situation or conditions change. Often, subordinates acting on the higher commander's intent develop the situation in ways that exploit unforeseen opportunities. *Commander's intent* is a clear and concise expression of the purpose of the operation and the desired military end state that supports mission command, provides focus to the staff, and helps subordinate and supporting commanders act to achieve the commander's desired results without further orders, even when the operation does not unfold as planned (JP 3-0). Mission command requires commanders to convey a clear commander's intent and concept of operations. These become essential in operations where multiple operational and mission variables interact with the lethal application of ground combat power. Such dynamic interaction often compels subordinate commanders to make difficult decisions in unforeseen circumstances.

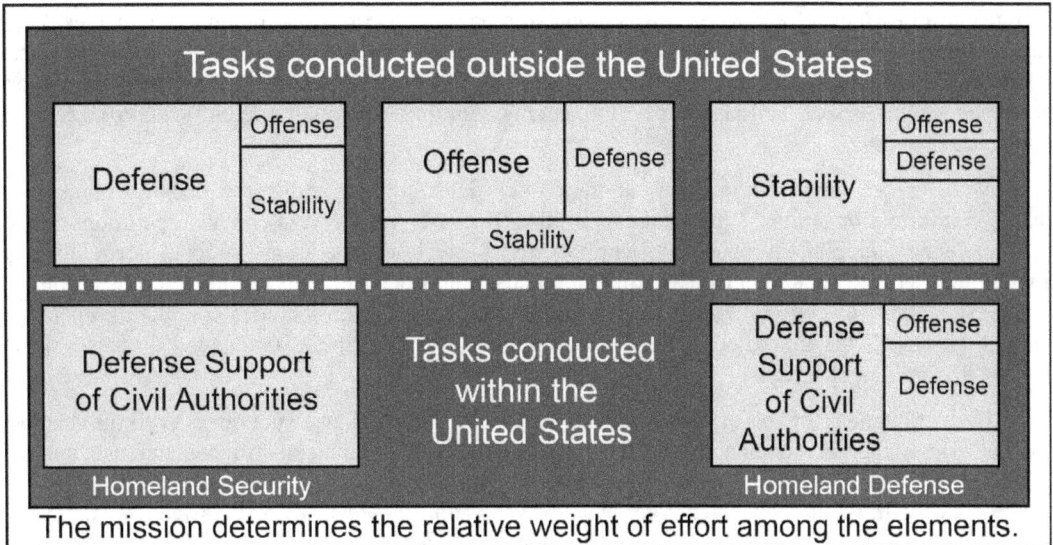

Figure 2-1. Decisive action

2-11. The operational concept addresses more than combat between armed opponents. Army forces conduct operations amid populations. This requires Army forces to defeat the enemy and simultaneously shape civil conditions. Offensive and defensive tasks defeat enemy forces whereas stability tasks shape civil conditions. Winning battles and engagements is important but alone may not be the most significant. Shaping civil conditions (in concert with civilian organizations, civil authorities, and multinational forces) often proves just as important to campaign success. In many joint operations, stability or defense support of civil authorities tasks often prove more important than offensive and defensive tasks.

2-12. The emphasis on different elements of decisive action changes with echelon, time, and location. In an operation dominated by stability, part of the force might conduct simultaneous offensive and defensive tasks in support of establishing stability. Within the United States, defense support of civil authorities may be the only activity actually conducted. In short, no single element is always more important than the others. Rather, simultaneous combinations of the elements, which commanders constantly adapt to conditions, are the key to successful land operations in achieving the end state.

2-13. Operations require versatile, adaptive units and tough, flexible leadership. These qualities develop first and foremost from training that prepares individuals and units for challenging operational environments. Managing training for unified land operations challenges leaders at all echelons. Training for offensive and defensive tasks develops discipline, endurance, unit cohesion, tolerance for uncertainty, and mutual support. It prepares Soldiers and units to address ambiguities inherent in stability and defense support of civil authorities tasks as well.

2-14. However, operational experience demonstrates that forces trained exclusively for offensive and defensive tasks are not as proficient at stability tasks as those trained specifically for stability tasks. For maximum effectiveness, tasks for stability and defense support of civil authorities require dedicated training, similar to training for offensive and defensive tasks. Likewise, forces involved in protracted stability or defense support of civil authorities require intensive training to regain proficiency in offensive or defensive tasks before engaging in large-scale combat operations. Effective training reflects a balance among the elements of decisive action that produce and sustain proficiency in all the tasks.

Purpose of Simultaneity

2-15. Simultaneously conducting offensive, defensive, and stability or defense support of civil authorities tasks requires the synchronized application of combat power. Simultaneity means doing multiple things at the same time. It requires the ability to conduct operations in depth and to integrate them so that their timing multiplies their effectiveness throughout an area of operations. Commanders consider their entire area of operations, the enemy, and information collection activities necessary to shape an operational environment and civil conditions. Then they mount simultaneous operations that immobilize, suppress, or shock the enemy. Such actions nullify the enemy's ability to conduct their synchronized, mutually supporting reactions.

2-16. Army forces increase the depth of their operations in time and space through combined arms, advanced information systems, and joint capabilities. Because Army forces conduct operations across large areas, the enemy faces many potential friendly actions. Executing operations in depth is equally important in wide area security; commanders act to keep threats from operating outside the reach of friendly forces. In defense support of civil authorities and some stability tasks, depth includes conducting operations that reach all citizens in the area of operations, bringing relief, as well as hope. (Chapter 4 discusses depth as an element of operational design.)

2-17. The simultaneity of the offense, defense, and stability or defense support of civil authorities is not absolute. The higher the echelon, the greater the possibility of simultaneous offense, defense, and stability. At lower echelons, an assigned task may require all of the echelons' combat power to execute a specific task. As an example, a higher echelon, such as a division, always performs offensive, defensive, and stability tasks in some form. Subordinate brigades perform some combination of offensive, defensive, and stability tasks but perhaps not all three simultaneously. For any organization assigned an area of operations, there will always be implied or even specified minimum essential stability tasks. If the organization cannot perform these tasks on its own, it must either request additional resources from higher headquarters or request relief from those tasks.

Tasks of Decisive Action

2-18. Decisive action requires simultaneous combinations of offense, defense, and stability or defense support of civil authorities tasks. Table 2-1 lists the tasks associated with each element and the purposes of each task. Each task has numerous associated subordinate tasks. When combined with who (unit), when (time), where (location), and why (purpose), the tasks may become mission statements.

Offensive Tasks

2-19. **An *offensive task* is a task conducted to defeat and destroy enemy forces and seize terrain, resources, and population centers.** Offensive tasks impose the commander's will on the enemy. In combined arms maneuver, the offense is a task of decisive action. Against a capable, adaptive enemy, the offense is the most direct and a sure means of seizing, retaining, and exploiting the initiative to gain physical and psychological advantages and achieve definitive results. In the offense, the decisive operation is a sudden, shattering action against an enemy weakness that capitalizes on speed, surprise, and shock. If that operation does not destroy the enemy, operations continue until enemy forces disintegrate or retreat to where they no longer pose a threat. Executing offensive tasks compels the enemy to react, creating or revealing additional weaknesses that the attacking force can exploit. (See Army tactics doctrine for a detailed discussion on offensive tasks.)

Table 2-1. Tasks of decisive action

Offense	*Defense*
Tasks:	**Tasks:**
• Movement to contact • Attack • Exploitation • Pursuit	• Mobile defense • Area defense • Retrograde
Purposes:	**Purposes:**
• Dislocate, isolate, disrupt, and destroy enemy forces • Seize key terrain • Deprive the enemy of resources • Develop intelligence • Deceive and divert the enemy • Create a secure environment for stability tasks	• Deter or defeat enemy offense • Gain time • Achieve economy of force • Retain key terrain • Protect the populace, critical assets, and infrastructure • Develop intelligence
Stability	*Defense Support of Civil Authorities*
Tasks:	**Tasks:**
• Establish civil security (including security force assistance) • Establish civil control • Restore essential services • Support to governance • Support to economic and infrastructure development	• Provide support for domestic disasters • Provide support for domestic chemical, biological, radiological, and nuclear incidents • Provide support for domestic civilian law enforcement agencies • Provide other designated support
Purposes:	**Purposes:**
• Provide a secure environment • Secure land areas • Meet the critical needs of the populace • Gain support for host-nation government • Shape the environment for interagency and host-nation success	• Save lives • Restore essential services • Maintain or restore law and order • Protect infrastructure and property • Maintain or restore local government • Shape the environment for interagency success

Defensive Tasks

2-20. **A *defensive task* is a task conducted to defeat an enemy attack, gain time, economize forces, and develop conditions favorable for offensive or stability tasks.** Normally the defense alone cannot achieve a decision. However, it can set conditions for a counteroffensive or counterattack that enables Army forces to regain the initiative. Defensive tasks can also establish a shield behind which wide area security can progress. Defensive tasks are a counter to the enemy offense. They defeat attacks, destroying as much of the attacking enemy as possible. They also preserve and maintain control over land, resources, and populations. The purpose of defensive tasks is to retain terrain, guard populations, and protect critical capabilities against enemy attacks. Commanders can conduct defensive tasks to gain time and economize forces so offensive tasks can be executed elsewhere. (See Army tactics doctrine for a detailed discussion on defensive tasks.)

Stability Tasks

2-21. Stability is an overarching term encompassing various military missions, tasks, and activities conducted outside the United States in coordination with other instruments of national power to maintain or reestablish a safe and secure environment, provide essential governmental services, emergency infrastructure reconstruction, and humanitarian relief. (See JP 3-0.) Army forces conduct stability tasks during both combined arms maneuver and wide area security. These tasks support a host-nation or an interim government or part of a transitional military authority when no government exists. Stability tasks involve both coercive and constructive actions. They help to establish or maintain a safe and secure environment and facilitate reconciliation among local or regional adversaries. Stability tasks can also help establish political, legal, social, and economic institutions while supporting the transition to legitimate host-nation governance. Stability tasks cannot succeed if they only react to enemy initiatives. Stability tasks must maintain the initiative by pursuing objectives that resolve the causes of instability. (See Army doctrine on stability tasks.)

Defense Support of Civil Authorities Tasks

2-22. Defense support of civil authorities is support provided by U.S. Federal military forces, Department of Defense civilians, Department of Defense contract personnel, Department of Defense component assets, and National Guard forces (when the Secretary of Defense, in coordination with the Governors of the affected States, elects and requests to use those forces in Title 32, U.S. Code, status). This support is in response to requests for assistance from civil authorities for domestic emergencies, law enforcement support, and other domestic activities, or from qualifying entities for special events. Defense support of civil authorities is a task that takes place only in the homeland, although some of its tasks are similar to stability tasks. Defense support of civil authorities is always conducted in support of another primary or lead federal agency and consists of four tasks (see table 2-1, page 2-5). National Guard forces in Title 32 or State active duty under the command and control of the Governor and the adjutant general are usually the first forces to respond on behalf of State authorities. When a lead federal agency ordered by the Secretary of Defense requests Title 10 forces to conduct a defense support of civil authorities mission, those forces are also under tight timelines and the command and control of the President, Secretary of Defense, and supported combatant commander. Unity of effort between the two responses is critical. (See JP 2-28 and Army doctrine on defense support of civil authorities.)

Homeland Defense and Decisive Action

2-23. *Homeland defense* is the protection of United States sovereignty, territory, domestic population, and critical defense infrastructure against external threats and aggression or other threats as directed by the President (JP 3-27). Department of Defense has lead responsibility for homeland defense while conducting defense support of civil authorities. Homeland defense operations conducted in the land domain could be the result of extraordinary circumstances and decisions by the President. In both homeland defense and defense support of civil authorities, Department of Defense and Army forces work closely with federal, state, and local agencies. Land domain homeland defense could consist of offensive and defensive tasks as part of decisive action. Given the lack of a conventional land threat and more transnational, hybrid threats, homeland defense in the land domain is more likely associated with the day-to-day steady-state support. Homeland defense provides this support to domestic partners and involves defending the homeland in depth using various means. These means may include support to civil law enforcement, antiterrorism and force protection, counterdrug, and other partners such as Canada and Mexico.

Information Collection in Decisive Action

2-24. *Information collection* is an activity that synchronizes and integrates the planning and employment of sensors and assets as well as the processing, exploitation, and dissemination systems in direct support of current and future operations (FM 3-55). It integrates the functions of the intelligence and operations staffs focused on answering the commander's critical information requirements. Joint operations refer to this as intelligence, surveillance, and reconnaissance (known as ISR). Information collection highlights aspects that influence how the Army operates as a ground force in close and continuous contact with the area of operations, including its weather, terrain, threat, and populace. At the tactical level, reconnaissance, surveillance, security, and intelligence operations are the primary means by which a commander plans, organizes, and executes shaping operations. These operations work to answer the commander's critical information requirements and support the decisive operation (see FM 3-55).

Transitioning in Decisive Action

2-25. Conducting decisive action involves more than simultaneous execution of all its tasks. It requires commanders and staffs to consider their units' capabilities and capacities relative to each task. Commanders consider their missions, decide which tactics to use, and balance the tasks of decisive action while preparing their commander's intent and concept of operations. They determine which tasks the force can accomplish simultaneously, if phasing is required, what additional resources it may need, and how to transition from one task to another.

2-26. The transitions between tasks of decisive action require careful assessment, prior planning, and unit preparation as commanders shift their combinations of offensive, defensive, stability, or defense support of civil authorities tasks. Commanders first assess the situation to determine applicable tasks and the priority for each. When conditions change, commanders adjust the combination of tasks of decisive action in the concept of operations. When an operation is phased, the plan includes these changes. The relative weight given to each element varies with the actual or anticipated conditions. It is reflected in tasks assigned to subordinates, resource allocation, and task organization.

2-27. Decisive action is not a phasing method. Commanders consider the concurrent conduct of each task—offensive, defensive, and stability or defense support of civil authorities—in every phase of an operation. Figure 2-2 illustrates combinations and weighting of the tasks of decisive action across the phases of a joint campaign or operation. The phases are examples. An actual campaign may name and array phases differently. (See JP 5-0 for a greater discussion on joint phasing.)

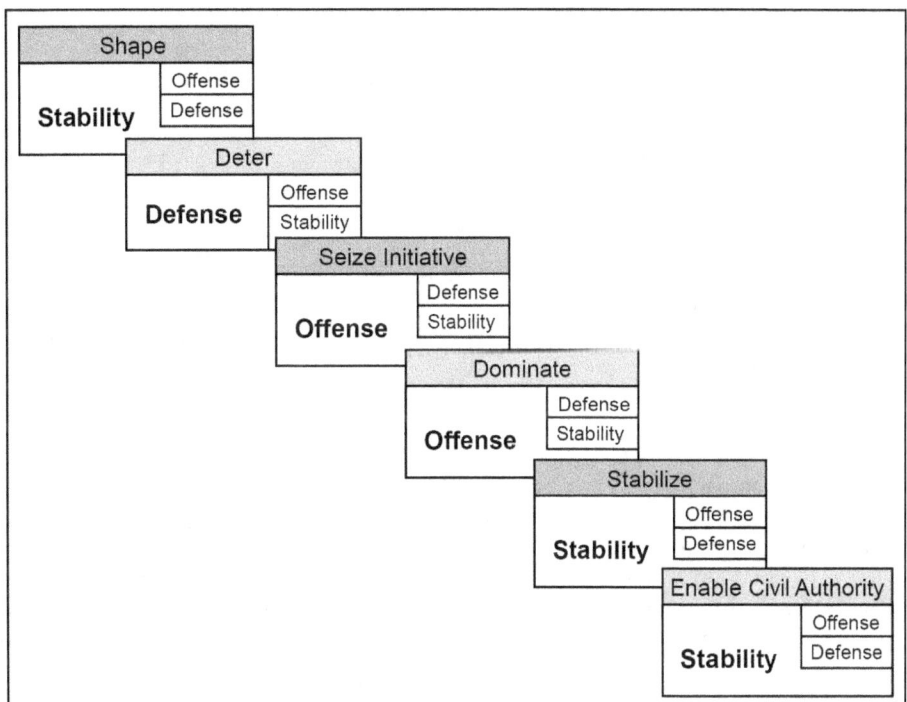

Figure 2-2. Example of combining the elements of decisive action in a notional campaign

2-28. Unanticipated changes in or an improved understanding of an operational environment may result in commanders reframing the problem and modifying operations to adapt to the changing situation. Unforeseen success in offense resulting in collapse of enemy opposition illustrates one unanticipated change. Another example is degradation in peace operations resulting in a requirement to transition to defensive tasks, or even offensive tasks, to reestablish stability. Commanders need to adjust the task organization to meet changing requirements. In some instances, they incorporate additional forces provided by higher headquarters to assist in the conduct of operations. When transitioning in operations, subordinate commanders clearly understand the higher commander's intent, concept of operations, and desired end state. Successful commanders understand which transitions involve risks, how much risk to accept, and where risk is accepted.

2-29. Seizing, retaining, and exploiting the initiative requires commanders to interpret developments and shift the weight of effort throughout their operations to achieve conclusive results. As they interpret, the assigned forces and priorities for each task of decisive action change. Throughout an operation, commanders constantly adapt and perform many tasks simultaneously. Commanders change tactics, modify their exercise of mission command, change task organization, and adjust the weight placed on each task of decisive action. These actions keep the force focused on accomplishing the mission, enabling it to seize, retain, and exploit the initiative. Commanders base each action on their understanding of the situation, available resources, and the force's ability to execute multiple, diverse tasks. After each action, commanders assess the results. Assessments include the progress of ongoing operations, changes in the situation, and effects the rules of engagement have on the force's effectiveness. Commanders not only assess how well a current operation is accomplishing the mission but also how its conduct is shaping the situation for subsequent missions.

2-30. Ultimately the operational concept of unified land operations aims to accomplish the mission. Execution of unified land operations through decisive action requires the following:

- A clear commander's intent and concept of operations that establishes the role of each element and its contribution to accomplishing the mission.
- A flexible mission command system.
- A shared understanding of an operational environment and purpose of the operation.
- Aggressive information collection and intelligence analysis.
- Aggressive security operations.
- Units that can quickly change their task organization.
- Operational and individual initiative.
- An ability to respond quickly.
- Responsive sustainment.
- Combat power applied through combined arms.
- Well-trained, cohesive teams and bold, adaptive, and imaginative leaders.
- The acceptance of prudent risk.
- An ability to liaise and coordinate operations with unified action partners within an operational environment.

ARMY CORE COMPETENCIES

2-31. Army forces demonstrate their core competencies of combined arms maneuver and wide area security by combining offensive, defensive, and stability or defense support of civil authorities tasks simultaneously. As part of a combined arms force within unified land operations, Army forces accept prudent risk to create opportunities to achieve decisive results. They employ synchronized action of lethal and nonlethal effects, proportional to the mission and informed by an understanding of an operational environment. Mission command that conveys commander's intent guides the adaptive use of Army forces.

2-32. Although distinct by definition, combined arms maneuver and wide area security are inseparable and simultaneous. Combined arms maneuver and wide area security provide the Army a focus for decisive action as well as a construct for understanding how Army forces use combined arms to achieve success in this contest of wills. As core competencies, combined arms maneuver and wide area security uniquely define what the Army provides to the joint force commander. Additionally, the Army is organized and equipped to support the joint force commander through combined arms to cover vast distances for extended periods. The Army works to integrate all available instruments to unified action partners to achieve the desired outcome.

2-33. Combined arms maneuver and wide area security are not tasks. They provide an operational context to assist a commander and staff in determining an operational approach and to combine tasks of decisive action into a coherent operation that assigns missions to subordinates. Forces execute these missions to defeat or destroy enemy forces, and seize or control areas vital to accomplishing their missions, while protecting civilians, infrastructure, and themselves. While all operations consist of simultaneous combined arms maneuver and wide area security in various proportions, most tactical tasks will be predominantly characterized by one or the other. The preponderant core competency determines the choice of defeat or stability mechanisms to describe how friendly forces accomplish the assigned mission. Generally, defeat mechanisms are appropriate for combined arms maneuver, while stability mechanisms are best suited for wide area security.

Combined Arms Maneuver

2-34. *Combined arms maneuver* is the application of the elements of combat power in unified action to defeat enemy ground forces; to seize, occupy, and defend land areas; and to achieve physical, temporal, and psychological advantages over the enemy to seize and exploit the initiative (ADP 3-0). Physical advantages may include control of key terrain, population centers, or critical resources and enablers. Temporal advantages enable Army forces to set the tempo and momentum of operations and decide when to fight so the enemy loses the ability to respond effectively. Psychological advantages impose fear, uncertainty, and doubt on the enemy, which serves to dissuade or disrupt the enemy's further planning and action.

2-35. Combined arms maneuver exposes enemies to friendly combat power from unexpected directions and denies them the ability to respond effectively. Combined arms maneuver throws the enemy off balance, follows up rapidly to prevent recovery, and destroys the enemy's will to fight. In addition, forces conducting combined arms maneuver threaten enemies indirectly, causing them to reveal their intentions and expose hidden vulnerabilities. Combined arms maneuver primarily employs defeat mechanisms against enemies and is dominated by offensive and defensive tasks.

2-36. **A *defeat mechanism* is a method through which friendly forces accomplish their mission against enemy opposition.** Army forces at all echelons use combinations of four defeat mechanisms: destroy, dislocate, disintegrate, and isolate. Applying focused combinations produces complementary and reinforcing effects not attainable with a single mechanism. Used individually, a defeat mechanism achieves results proportional to the effort expended. Used in combination, the effects are likely to be both synergistic and lasting. When commanders destroy, they apply lethal combat power on an enemy capability so that it can no longer perform any function. The enemy cannot restore it to a usable condition without being entirely rebuilt. Commanders dislocate by employing forces to obtain significant positional advantage, rendering the enemy's dispositions less valuable, perhaps even irrelevant. Disintegrate means to disrupt the enemy's command and control system, degrading its ability to conduct operations. This action leads to a rapid collapse of the enemy's capabilities or will to fight. When commanders isolate, they deny an enemy or adversary access to capabilities that enable the exercise of coercion, influence, potential advantage, and freedom of action.

2-37. Commanders describe a defeat mechanism as the physical, temporal, or psychological effects it produces. Defeat mechanisms are not tactical missions; rather, they describe broad operational and tactical effects. Commanders translate these effects into tactical tasks. Operational art formulates the most effective, efficient way to defeat enemy aims. Physically defeating the enemy deprives enemy forces of the ability to achieve those aims. Temporally defeating the enemy anticipates enemy reactions and counters them before they can become effective. Psychologically defeating the enemy deprives the enemy of the will to continue the fight.

2-38. Combined arms maneuver causes the enemy to confront dangers faster than the enemy can respond to them. For example, in forcible entry operations, effective combined arms maneuver defeats antiaccess and area denial efforts, disrupting the enemy and allowing the ground force to transition rapidly to stability tasks. In operations dominated by stability tasks, commanders employ combined arms maneuver to interpose friendly forces between the population and threats to security. This positioning denies sanctuary to the enemy and fosters stability to populations. Army forces follow up rapidly to prevent recovery and reconstitution while continuing operations to destroy the enemy's will to fight.

Wide Area Security

2-39. *Wide area security* is the application of the elements of combat power in unified action to protect populations, forces, infrastructure, and activities; to deny the enemy positions of advantage; and to consolidate gains in order to retain the initiative (ADP 3-0). Army forces conduct security tasks to provide the joint force commander with reaction time and maneuver space. Additionally, these forces defeat or fix the enemy before the enemy can attack, thus allowing the commander to retain the initiative.

2-40. As part of unified land operations, Army forces may assist the development of host-nation security forces, a viable market economy, the rule of law, and an effective government by establishing and maintaining security in an area of operations. The goal is a stable civil situation sustainable by host-nation assets without Army forces. Security, the health of the local economy, and the capability of self-government are related. Without security, the local economy falters, populations feel unsecure, and enemy forces gain an advantage. A functioning economy provides employment and reduces the dependence of the population on the military for necessities. Security and economic stability precede an effective and stable government.

2-41. Wide area security includes the minimum essential stability tasks as part of decisive action. Army forces perform five primary stability tasks:

- Establish civil security, including security force assistance.
- Establish civil control.
- Restore essential services.
- Support governance.
- Support economic and infrastructure development.

2-42. The combination of stability tasks conducted during operations depends on the situation. In some operations, the host nation can meet most or all of the population's requirements. In those cases, Army forces work with and through host-nation authorities. Commanders use civil affairs operations to mitigate how the military presence affects the populace and vice versa. Conversely, Army forces operating in a failed state may need to support the well-being of the local populace. That situation requires Army forces to work with civilian organizations to restore basic capabilities. Again, civil affairs operations prove essential in establishing trust between Army forces and civilian organizations required for effective, working relationships.

2-43. A *stability mechanism* is the primary method through which friendly forces affect civilians in order to attain conditions that support establishing a lasting, stable peace. As with defeat mechanisms, combinations of stability mechanisms produce complementary and reinforcing effects that accomplish the mission more effectively and efficiently than single mechanisms do alone.

2-44. The four stability mechanisms are compel, control, influence, and support. Compel means to use, or threaten to use, lethal force to establish control and dominance, effect behavioral change, or enforce compliance with mandates, agreements, or civil authority. Control involves imposing civil order. Influence means to alter the opinions, attitudes, and ultimately behavior of foreign friendly, neutral, adversary, and enemy populations through inform and influence activities, presence, and conduct. Support is to establish, reinforce, or set the conditions necessary for the instruments of national power to function effectively.

MISSION COMMAND

2-45. Mission command is the exercise of authority and direction by the commander using mission orders to enable disciplined initiative within the commander's intent to empower agile and adaptive leaders in the conduct of unified land operations (see Army doctrine on mission command). Exercised by Army commanders, it blends the art of command and the science of control while integrating the warfighting functions to conduct the tasks of decisive action. Mission command has six fundamental principles (see Army doctrine on mission command for detailed discussion of fundamental principles):

- Build cohesive teams through mutual trust.
- Create shared understanding.
- Provide a clear commander's intent.
- Exercise disciplined initiative.
- Use mission orders.
- Accept prudent risk.

2-46. As a philosophy, mission command is essential to the Army's core competencies. Mission command illuminates the Army leader's responsibility to understand, visualize, describe, direct, lead, and assess. It provides commanders and staff with a philosophy for operating in an uncertain environment as opposed to trying to create certainty and impose order and control over a situation. Mission command recognizes that Army leaders command not only Army forces but also work with diverse unified action partners. (See chapter 3 for a discussion of mission command as a warfighting function.)

2-47. Mission command emphasizes the critical contributions of leaders at every echelon. It establishes a mindset among Army leaders that the best understanding comes from a synthesis of information and an understanding from all echelons and unified action partners—bottom-up input is as important as top-down guidance. Mission command emphasizes the importance of creating shared understanding and purpose. It highlights how commanders—through disciplined initiative within the commander's intent—transition among offensive, defensive, and stability or defense support of civil authorities tasks and vary the level of control to account for changes in an operational environment.

2-48. Mission command is the overarching term for both the warfighting function and the philosophy of command. Mission command guides Army leaders how to think about what subordinate leaders and their Soldiers do to conduct successful operations on land. By emphasizing people as the driving force behind the development of technology, mission command adapts technology to human needs, not humans to technological restrictions. Understanding and influencing people to achieve success in unified land operations are fundamental to how the commander exercises the art of command.

2-49. Successful mission command fosters adaptability and a greater understanding of an operational environment. Adaptability reflects a quality that Army leaders and forces exhibit through critical thinking, their comfort with ambiguity and uncertainty, their willingness to accept prudent risk, and their ability to rapidly adjust while continuously assessing the situation. A greater understanding enables commanders to make better decisions and develop courses of action that more quickly accomplish missions and achieve the overall end state.

Art of Command

2-50. *Command* is the authority that a commander in the armed forces lawfully exercises over subordinates by virtue of rank or assignment. Command includes the authority and responsibility for effectively using available resources and for planning the employment of, organizing, directing, coordinating, and controlling military forces for the accomplishment of assigned missions. It also includes responsibility for health, welfare, morale, and discipline of assigned personnel (JP 1).

2-51. Command is considered more art than science because it depends on actions only humans can perform. The art of command is the creative and skillful exercise of authority by commanders through decisionmaking and leadership. Enabled by a mission command system, commanders synthesize and apply this knowledge across all levels of command. They gather knowledge from all levels—higher, lower, and lateral—as well as outside the military. (See Army doctrine on mission command for a discussion of a mission command system.) Those in command have authority, decisionmaking skills, and leadership abilities.

2-52. Authority is the delegated power to judge, act, or command. It includes responsibility, accountability, and delegation. Commanders rely on their education, experience, knowledge, and judgment in applying authority as they decide (plan how to achieve the end state) and lead (direct their forces during preparation and execution). The authority of command provides the basis for control. Leaders who use command authority strive to do so with firmness, care, and skill.

2-53. Decisionmaking skills refer to the ability to select a course of action as the one most favorable to accomplish the mission. Commanders apply knowledge to the situation thus translating their visualization into action. Decisionmaking includes knowing whether to decide or not, when and what to decide, and the consequences. Commanders understand, visualize, describe, and direct to determine and communicate their commander's intent, concept of operations, commander's critical information requirements, and desired end state.

2-54. Leadership abilities refer to the ability to influence people by providing purpose, direction, and motivation, while operating to accomplish the mission and improve the organization. A commander leads through a combination of personal example, persuasion, and compulsion. (See Army doctrine on leadership.)

Science of Control

2-55. While command is a commander's personal function, control involves the entire force. Staffs exercise the science of control with their commander's oversight. In the context of mission command, control is the regulation of forces and warfighting functions to accomplish the mission in accordance with the commander's intent. Commanders require control to direct operations. Aided by staffs, commanders exercise control over all forces in their area of operations. Staffs coordinate, synchronize, and integrate actions, inform the commander, and exercise control for the commander.

2-56. The control aspect of mission command applies more science or technical aspects than art because it relies on objectivity, facts, empirical methods, and analysis. The science of control includes the detailed systems and procedures to improve the commander's understanding and support accomplishing missions. Commanders and staffs use the science of control to overcome or mitigate the physical and procedural constraints under which units operate. Control demands commanders and staffs to understand those aspects of operations that they can analyze and measure. These include the physical capabilities and limitations of friendly and enemy organizations and systems as well as other aspects of operational environments. Control also requires a realistic appreciation for time-distance factors and the time required to initiate certain actions. Commanders apply only the degree of control necessary to ensure mission accomplishment. The science of control supports the art of command.

TENETS OF UNIFIED LAND OPERATIONS

2-57. The tenets of unified land operations describe the Army's approach to generating and applying combat power in campaigns and major operations. A *campaign* is a series of related major operations aimed at achieving strategic and operational objectives within a given time and space (JP 5-0). A *major operation* is a series of tactical actions (battles, engagements, strikes) conducted by combat forces of a single or several Services, coordinated in time and place, to achieve strategic or operational objectives in an operational area (JP 3-0). A single joint force commander conducts these actions simultaneously or sequentially according to a common plan. Subordinate Service and functional component commanders (and joint force commanders when subordinate joint forces are established) command and control their forces executing the campaign's major operations.

2-58. For Army forces, an operation is a military action, consisting of two of more related tactical actions, designed to achieve a strategic objective, in whole or in part. A tactical action is a battle or engagement employing lethal and nonlethal actions designed for a specific purpose relative to the enemy, the terrain, friendly forces, or other entity. Tactical actions include widely varied activities. They can include an attack to seize a piece of terrain or destroy an enemy unit, the defense of a population, and the training of other militaries to assist security forces as part of building partner capacity. Army operations are characterized by six tenets:

- Flexibility.
- Integration.
- Lethality.
- Adaptability.
- Depth.
- Synchronization.

FLEXIBILITY

2-59. To achieve tactical, operational, and strategic success, commanders seek to demonstrate flexibility in spite of adversity. They employ a versatile mix of capabilities, formations, and equipment for conducting operations. Flexibility is an important trait of effective leaders. Commanders enable adaptive forces through flexibility, which facilitates collaborative planning and decentralized execution. They exercise mission command to achieve maximum flexibility and foster individual initiative. To adapt, leaders constantly learn from experience (their own and that of others) and apply new knowledge to each situation. Flexible plans help units adapt quickly to changing circumstances in operations. Commanders build opportunities for initiative by anticipating events that allow them to operate inside of the enemy's decision cycle or react promptly to deteriorating situations.

2-60. Flexibility and innovation are at a premium, as are creative and adaptive leaders. As knowledge increases, the Army continuously adapts to changes in an operational environment. Such adaptation enhances flexibility across the range of military operations. The Army requires flexibility in thought, plans, and operations to be successful in unified land operations.

INTEGRATION

2-61. Army forces do not operate independently but as a part of a larger unified action. Army leaders integrate Army operations within this larger effort. Through the mission command warfighting function, commanders, assisted by their staffs, integrate numerous processes and activities within the headquarters and across the force. Integration involves efforts to exercise inform and influence activities with unified action partners and efforts to conform Army capabilities and plans to the larger concept. Commanders extend the depth of operations through joint integration.

2-62. When determining an operation's depth, commanders consider their own capabilities as well as joint capabilities and limitations. They use these capabilities to ensure actions executed at an operational depth receive robust and uninterrupted support. Commanders sequence and synchronize operations in time and space to achieve simultaneous effects throughout an operational area. Army leaders seek to use Army capabilities to complement those of their unified action partners; they depend on those partners to provide capabilities that supplement or are not organic to Army forces. Effective integration requires creating shared understanding and purpose through collaboration with unified action partners.

LETHALITY

2-63. Effective decisive action relies on lethality. The capacity for physical destruction is a foundation of all other military capabilities, the most basic building block for military operations. Army leaders organize, equip, train, and employ their formations for unmatched lethality under a wide range of conditions. Lethality is a persistent requirement for Army organizations, even in conditions where only the implicit threat of violence suffices to accomplish the mission through nonlethal engagements and activities.

2-64. An inherent, complementary relationship exists between using lethal force and applying military capabilities for nonlethal purposes. Though each situation requires a different mix of violence and constraint, lethal and nonlethal actions used together complement each other and create dilemmas for opponents. Lethal actions are critical to accomplishing offensive and defensive tasks. However, nonlethal actions are also important contributors to combined arms operations, regardless of which element of decisive action dominates. Finding ways to accomplish the mission with an appropriate mix of lethal and nonlethal actions remains an important consideration for every commander.

ADAPTABILITY

2-65. Adaptability reflects a quality that Army leaders and forces exhibit through critical thinking, their comfort with ambiguity and uncertainty, their willingness to accept prudent risk, and their ability to rapidly adjust while continuously assessing the situation. They accept that no prefabricated solutions to problems exist. Army leaders adapt their thinking, their formations, and their employment techniques to the specific situations they face.

2-66. Effective units adapt. Adaptability is essential to seizing, retaining, and exploiting the initiative based on relevant understanding of the specific situation. For example, leaders demonstrate adaptability while adjusting the balance of lethal and nonlethal actions necessary to achieve a position of relative advantage and set conditions for conflict resolution within their areas of operations. Transitions between operations, whether anticipated or unanticipated, also demonstrate adaptability as leaders cope with changes in an operational environment. These leaders enable adaptive forces through flexible, collaborative planning and decentralized execution. Adaptability results in teams that—

- Anticipate transitions.
- Accept risks to create opportunities.
- Influence all partners.

DEPTH

2-67. Depth is the extension of operations in time, space, or purpose, including deep-close-security operations, to achieve definitive results. Army leaders strike enemy forces throughout their depth, preventing the effective employment of reserves, command and control nodes, logistics, and other capabilities not in direct contact with friendly forces. Operations in depth can disrupt the enemy's decision cycle. These operations contribute to protecting the force by destroying enemy capabilities before the enemy can use them. Commanders balance their forces' tempo and momentum to produce simultaneous results throughout their operational areas. To achieve simultaneity, commanders establish a higher tempo to target enemy capabilities located at the limit of a force's operational reach.

2-68. Executing operations in depth is equally important when performing stability tasks. Commanders act to keep threats from operating outside the reach of friendly forces. Unified land operations achieves the best results when the enemy must cope with U.S. actions throughout the enemy's entire physical, temporal, and organizational depth. Army forces use combined arms, advanced information systems, and joint capabilities to increase the depth of friendly operations.

SYNCHRONIZATION

2-69. *Synchronization* is the arrangement of military actions in time, space, and purpose to produce maximum relative combat power at a decisive place and time (JP 2-0). It is the ability to execute multiple related and mutually supporting tasks in different locations at the same time, producing greater effects than executing each in isolation. For example, synchronization of information collection, obstacles, direct fires, and indirect fires results in the destruction of an enemy formation. When conducting offensive tasks, synchronizing forces along multiple lines of operations temporarily disrupts the enemy organization and allows for exploitation.

2-70. Information networks greatly enhance the potential for synchronization. They do this by allowing commanders to quickly understand an operational environment and communicate their commander's intent. Subordinate and adjacent units use that common understanding to synchronize their actions with those of other units without direct control from the higher headquarters. Information networks do not guarantee synchronization; however, they provide a powerful tool for leaders to use in synchronizing their efforts.

2-71. Commanders determine the degree of control necessary to synchronize their operations. They balance synchronization with agility and initiative, never surrendering the initiative for the sake of synchronization. Rather, they synchronize activities to best facilitate mission accomplishment. Excessive synchronization can lead to too much control, which limits the initiative of subordinates and undermines mission command.

Chapter 3

Combat Power

This chapter discusses combat power in detail. It first discusses the elements of combat power. Then it discusses the six warfighting functions: mission command, movement and maneuver, intelligence, fires, sustainment, and protection. Lastly, this chapter discusses the means of organizing combat power.

THE ELEMENTS OF COMBAT POWER

3-1. Combined arms maneuver and wide area security, executed through simultaneous offensive, defensive, stability, or defense support of civil authorities tasks, require continuously generating and applying combat power, often for extended periods. *Combat power* **is the total means of destructive, constructive, and information capabilities that a military unit or formation can apply at a given time**. Army forces generate combat power by converting potential into effective action.

3-2. To execute combined arms operations, commanders conceptualize capabilities in terms of combat power. Combat power has eight elements: leadership, information, mission command, movement and maneuver, intelligence, fires, sustainment, and protection. The Army collectively describes the last six elements as the warfighting functions. Commanders apply combat power through the warfighting functions using leadership and information. (See figure 3-1.)

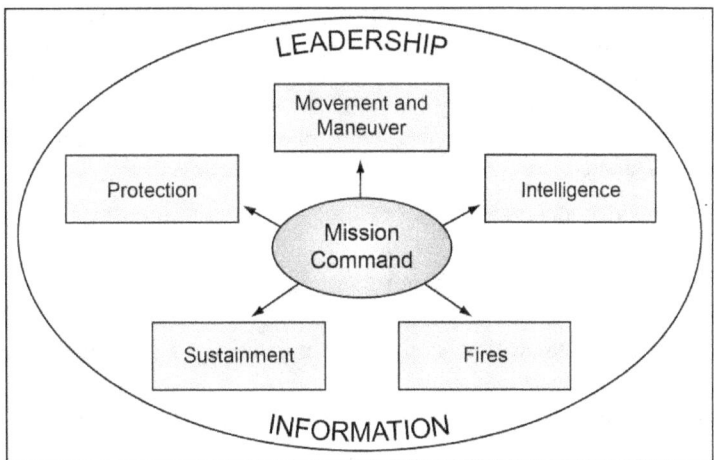

Figure 3-1. The elements of combat power

3-3. Generating and maintaining combat power throughout an operation is essential to success. Factors contributing to generating combat power include employing reserves, rotating committed forces, and focusing joint support. Commanders balance the ability to mass lethal and nonlethal effects with the need to deploy and sustain the units that produce those effects. They balance the ability of accomplishing the mission with the ability to project and sustain the force.

3-4. Commanders apply leadership through mission command. Leadership is the multiplying and unifying element of combat power. The Army defines leadership as the process of influencing people by providing purpose, direction, and motivation, while operating to accomplish the mission and improve the organization. (See FM 6-22 for a detailed discussion of leadership.) An Army leader, by virtue of assumed role or assigned responsibility, inspires and influences people to accomplish organizational goals.

3-5. Information enables commanders at all levels to make informed decisions on how best to apply combat power. Ultimately, this creates opportunities to achieve definitive results. Knowledge management enables commanders to make informed, timely decisions despite the uncertainty of operations. Information management helps commanders make and disseminate effective decisions faster than the enemy can. Every operation requires complementary tasks of inform and influence activities that affect the commander's intent and concept of operations. Every operation also requires cyber electromagnetic activities. These activities ensure information availability, protection, and delivery as well as a means to deny, degrade, or disrupt the enemy's use of its command and control systems and other cyber capabilities. Commanders use information and a mission command system to understand, visualize, describe, and direct operations.

THE SIX WARFIGHTING FUNCTIONS

3-6. Commanders use the warfighting functions to help them exercise command and to help them and their staffs exercise control. A *warfighting function* is a group of tasks and systems (people, organizations, information, and processes) united by a common purpose that commanders use to accomplish missions and training objectives. All warfighting functions possess scalable capabilities to mass lethal and nonlethal effects. The Army's warfighting functions link directly to the joint functions.

MISSION COMMAND WARFIGHTING FUNCTION

3-7. The *mission command warfighting function* is the related tasks and systems that develop and integrate those activities enabling a commander to balance the art of command and the science of control in order to integrate the other warfighting functions. Commanders, assisted by their staffs, integrate numerous processes and activities within the headquarters and across the force as they exercise mission command.

3-8. Mission command encourages the greatest possible freedom of action from subordinates. While the commander remains the central figure in mission command, it enables subordinates to develop the situation. Through disciplined initiative in dynamic conditions within the commander's intent, subordinates adapt and act decisively. Mission command creates a shared understanding of an operational environment and the commander's intent to establish the appropriate degree of control. Collaborative engagement among commanders, staffs, and unified action partners helps clarify the meaning of events or situations embedded in their unique and continually evolving operational environment. They share information, knowledge, perceptions, and concepts regardless of physical location.

3-9. The art of command is the creative and skillful exercise of authority through decisionmaking and leadership. As commanders exercise the art of command, they perform the following tasks:
- Drive the operations process through their activities of understanding, visualizing, describing, directing, leading, and assessing operations.
- Develop teams, both within their own organizations and with joint, interagency, and multinational partners.
- Inform and influence audiences, inside and outside their organizations.

3-10. The commander leads the staff's tasks under the science of control. The science of control consists of systems and procedures to improve the commander's understanding and to support accomplishing missions. The four primary staff tasks are:
- Conduct the operations process: plan, prepare, execute, and assess.
- Conduct knowledge management and information management.
- Conduct inform and influence activities.
- Conduct cyber electromagnetic activities.

3-11. In addition to mission command warfighting function tasks, five additional tasks reside within the mission command warfighting function. These tasks are:
- Conduct military deception.
- Conduct civil affairs operations.
- Install, operate, and maintain the network.

- Conduct airspace control.
- Conduct information protection.

As much as the commander leads the staff's tasks, the staff tasks fully support the commander in executing the commander's tasks. Commanders and staffs, work with unified action partners to perform mission command warfighting function tasks that contribute to mission accomplishment.

3-12. *Inform and influence activities* **is the integration of designated information-related capabilities in order to synchronize themes, messages, and actions with operations to inform United States and global audiences, influence foreign audiences, and affect adversary and enemy decisionmaking.** As a primary staff task under mission command, conduct inform and influence activities aids the commander to inform domestic and friendly audiences. It enables the commander to develop and maintain relationships with partners and influence adversary and enemy decisionmaking to gain an operational advantage.

3-13. All assets and capabilities at a commander's disposal have the capacity to inform and influence audiences at varying degrees. Called information-related capabilities, these tools and techniques use a dimension within an information environment to generate a desired end state. When properly integrated, information-related capabilities enhance and reinforce mission objectives, giving the commander an information advantage. The commander designates the primary information-related capabilities of inform and influence activities: public affairs, military information support operations, and Soldier and leader engagements.

3-14. *Cyber electromagnetic activities* **are activities leveraged to seize, retain, and exploit an advantage over adversaries and enemies in both cyberspace and the electromagnetic spectrum, while simultaneously denying and degrading adversary and enemy use of the same and protecting the mission command system.** Cyber electromagnetic activities consist of cyberspace operations, electronic warfare, and electromagnetic spectrum operations. These activities can employ the same technologies, capabilities, and enablers to accomplish assigned tasks. Commanders integrate and synchronize cyber electromagnetic activities across all command echelons and warfighting functions as part of the operations process.

MOVEMENT AND MANEUVER WARFIGHTING FUNCTION

3-15. The *movement and maneuver warfighting function* **is the related tasks and systems that move and employ forces to achieve a position of relative advantage over the enemy and other threats.** Direct fire and close combat are inherent in maneuver. The movement and maneuver warfighting function includes tasks associated with force projection related to gaining a position of advantage over the enemy. Movement is necessary to disperse and displace the force as a whole or in part when maneuvering. Maneuver is the employment of forces in the operational area. It works through movement and with fires to achieve a position of advantage relative to the enemy to accomplish the mission. Commanders use maneuver for massing the effects of combat power to achieve surprise, shock, and momentum. Effective maneuver requires close coordination with fires. Both tactical and operational maneuver require sustainment support. The movement and maneuver warfighting function includes the following tasks:

- Deploy.
- Move.
- Maneuver.
- Employ direct fires.
- Occupy an area.
- Conduct mobility and countermobility operations.
- Conduct reconnaissance and surveillance.
- Employ battlefield obscuration.

3-16. The movement and maneuver warfighting function does not include administrative movements of personnel and materiel. These movements fall under the sustainment warfighting function. FM 3-35 discusses force projection.

INTELLIGENCE WARFIGHTING FUNCTION

3-17. The *intelligence warfighting function* **is the related tasks and systems that facilitate understanding the enemy, terrain, and civil considerations**. This warfighting function includes understanding threats, adversaries, and weather. It synchronizes information collection with the primary tactical tasks of reconnaissance, surveillance, security, and intelligence operations. Intelligence is driven by commanders and is more than just collection. Developing intelligence is a continuous process that involves analyzing information from all sources and conducting operations to develop the situation. The warfighting function includes specific intelligence and communication structures at each echelon. The intelligence warfighting function includes the following tasks:

- Support force generation.
- Support situational understanding.
- Provide intelligence support to targeting and information capabilities.
- Collect information.

3-18. The intelligence warfighting function provides specific intelligence capabilities and communication structures at each echelon from the national level through the tactical level. These capabilities and structures include intelligence organizations, systems, and procedures for generating intelligence reports. They also include products, visualization aides, situational understanding and awareness products, and other critical information products. Effective communication connectivity and automation are essential components of this architecture. (FM 2-0 discusses the intelligence warfighting function.)

FIRES WARFIGHTING FUNCTION

3-19. The *fires warfighting function* **is the related tasks and systems that provide collective and coordinated use of Army indirect fires, air and missile defense, and joint fires through the targeting process**. Army fires systems deliver fires in support of offensive and defensive tasks to create specific lethal and nonlethal effects on a target. The fires warfighting function includes the following tasks:

- Deliver fires.
- Integrate all forms of Army, joint, and multinational fires.
- Conduct targeting.

SUSTAINMENT WARFIGHTING FUNCTION

3-20. The *sustainment warfighting function* **is the related tasks and systems that provide support and services to ensure freedom of action, extend operational reach, and prolong endurance**. The endurance of Army forces is primarily a function of their sustainment. Sustainment determines the depth and duration of Army operations. It is essential to retaining and exploiting the initiative. Sustainment provides the support necessary to maintain operations until mission accomplishment. The sustainment warfighting function includes the following tasks:

- Conduct logistics.
- Provide personnel services.
- Provide health service support.

Logistics

3-21. Logistics is planning and executing the movement and support of forces. It includes those aspects of military operations that—

- Design, develop, acquire, store, move, distribute, maintain, evacuate, and dispose of materiel.
- Acquire or build, maintain, operate, and dispose of facilities.
- Acquire or furnish services.

3-22. Although joint doctrine defines it as science, logistics involves both military art and science. Knowing when and how to accept risk, prioritizing a myriad of requirements, and balancing limited resources all require military art. Logistics integrates strategic, operational, and tactical support of deployed forces while scheduling the mobilization and deployment of additional forces and materiel. Logistics includes—

- Maintenance.
- Transportation.
- Supply.
- Field services.
- Distribution.
- Operational contract support.
- General engineering support.

Personnel Services

3-23. Personnel services are those sustainment functions related to Soldiers' welfare, readiness, and quality of life. Personnel services complement logistics by planning for and coordinating efforts that provide and sustain personnel. Personnel services include—

- Human resources support.
- Financial management.
- Legal support.
- Religious support.
- Band support.

Health Service Support

3-24. The Army Health System is a component of the military health system that oversees operational management of the health service support and force health protection missions. The Army Health System includes all mission support services performed, provided, and arranged by the Army Medical Department to support health service support and force health protection mission requirements for the Army. Health service support is part of the sustainment warfighting function while force health protection is a part of the protection warfighting function.

3-25. The health service support mission promotes, improves, conserves, or restores the mental and physical well being of Soldiers and, as directed, other personnel. This mission consists of casualty care, medical evacuation, and medical logistics. Casualty care encompasses the treatment aspects of a number of Army Medical Department functions including—

- Organic and area medical support.
- Hospitalization (to include treatment of chemical, biological, radiological, and nuclear patients).
- Dental treatment.
- Behavioral health and neuropsychiatric treatment.
- Clinical laboratory services.
- Medical evacuation (to include en-route care and medical regulating).
- Medical logistics (to include blood and blood products).

Health service support closely relates to force health protection, the measures to promote, improve, or conserve the mental and physical well-being of Soldiers. These measures enable a healthy and fit force, prevent injury and illness, and protect the force from health hazards. (FM 4-0 discusses the sustainment warfighting function, ATTP 4-02 discusses the Army Health System, and FM 1-0 covers human resources support.)

PROTECTION WARFIGHTING FUNCTION

3-26. The *protection warfighting function* is the related tasks and systems that preserve the force so the commander can apply maximum combat power to accomplish the mission. Preserving the force includes protecting personnel (combatants and noncombatants) and physical assets of the United States and multinational military and civilian partners, to include the host nation. The protection warfighting function enables the commander to maintain the force's integrity and combat power. Protection determines the degree to which potential threats can disrupt operations and then counters or mitigates those threats. Protection is a continuing activity; it integrates all protection capabilities to safeguard bases, secure routes, and protect forces. To ensure maintenance of the critical asset list and the defended asset list and associated resourcing of fixed sites and forces against air and indirect fire threats, air and missile defense participates in meetings geared to protection activities. The protection warfighting function includes the following tasks:

- Conduct operational area security.
- Employ safety techniques (including fratricide avoidance).
- Implement operations security.
- Implement physical security procedures.
- Provide intelligence support to protection.
- Implement information protection.
- Apply antiterrorism measures.
- Conduct law and order.
- Conduct survivability operations.
- Provide force health protection.
- Conduct chemical, biological, radiological, and nuclear operations.
- Provide explosive ordnance disposal and protection support.
- Coordinate air and missile defense.
- Conduct personnel recovery operations.
- Conduct internment and resettlement.

ORGANIZING COMBAT POWER

3-27. Commanders employ three means to organize combat power: force tailoring, task-organizing, and mutual support.

FORCE TAILORING

3-28. *Force tailoring* **is the process of determining the right mix of forces and the sequence of their deployment in support of a joint force commander.** It involves selecting the right force structure for a joint operation from available units within a combatant command or from the Army force pool. Commanders then sequence selected forces into the area of operations as part of force projection. Joint force commanders request and receive forces for each campaign phase, adjusting the quantity of Service component forces to match the weight of effort required. Army Service component commanders tailor Army forces to meet land force requirements determined by joint force commanders. Army Service component commanders also recommend forces and a deployment sequence to meet those requirements. Force tailoring is continuous. As new forces rotate into the area of operations, forces with excess capabilities return to the supporting combatant and Army Service component commands.

TASK-ORGANIZING

3-29. *Task-organizing* **is the act of designing an operating force, support staff, or sustainment package of specific size and composition to meet a unique task or mission.** Characteristics to examine when task-organizing the force include, but are not limited to, training, experience, equipment, sustainability, operational environment, enemy threat, and mobility. Task-organizing includes allocating assets to subordinate commanders and establishing their command and support relationships. It occurs within a tailored force package as commanders organize subordinate units for specific missions employing doctrinal command and support relationships. As task-organizing continues, commanders reorganize units for subsequent missions. The ability of Army forces to task-organize gives them extraordinary agility. It lets commanders configure their units to best use available resources. It also allows Army forces to match unit capabilities to the priority assigned to offensive, defensive, and stability or defense support of civil authorities tasks. The ability of sustainment forces to tailor and task-organize ensures commanders freedom of action to change as mission requirements dictate.

MUTUAL SUPPORT

3-30. Commanders consider mutual support when task-organizing forces, assigning areas of operations, and positioning units. *Mutual support* is that support which units render each other against an enemy, because of their assigned tasks, their position relative to each other and to the enemy, and their inherent capabilities (JP 3-31). In Army doctrine, mutual support is a planning consideration related to force disposition, not a command relationship. Mutual support has two aspects—supporting range and supporting distance. Understanding mutual support and accepting risk during operations are fundamental to the art of tactics.

3-31. *Supporting range* **is the distance one unit may be geographically separated from a second unit yet remain within the maximum range of the second unit's weapons systems.** It depends on available weapons systems and is normally the maximum range of the supporting unit's indirect fire weapons. For small units (such as squads, sections, and platoons), it is the distance between two units that their direct fires can cover effectively. Visibility may limit the supporting range. If one unit cannot effectively or safely fire in support of another, the first may not be in supporting range even though its weapons have the required range.

3-32. *Supporting distance* **is the distance between two units that can be traveled in time for one to come to the aid of the other and prevent its defeat by an enemy or ensure it regains control of a civil situation.** The following factors affect supporting distance:

- Terrain and mobility.
- Distance.
- Enemy capabilities.
- Friendly capabilities.
- Reaction time.

When friendly forces are static, supporting range equals supporting distance.

3-33. The capabilities of supported and supporting units affect supporting distance. Units may be within supporting distance, but if the supported unit cannot communicate with the supporting unit, the supporting unit may not be able to affect the operation's outcome. In such cases, the units are not within supporting distance, regardless of their proximity to each other. If the units share a common operational picture, the situation may differ greatly. Relative proximity may be less important than both units' abilities to coordinate their maneuver and fires. To exploit the advantage of supporting distance, the units have to synchronize their maneuver and fires more effectively than the enemy can. Otherwise, the enemy may be able to defeat both units in detail.

3-34. Commanders consider the supporting distance in operations dominated by stability or defense support of civil authorities tasks. Units maintain mutual support when one unit can draw on another's capabilities. An interdependent joint force may make proximity less significant than available capability. For example, Air Force assets may be able to move a preventive medicine detachment from an intermediate staging base to an operational area threatened by an epidemic. An additional treatment capability might be moved to the operational area based on the threat to Soldiers and the populace.

3-35. Commanders should be aware that conventional land forces and special operations forces may operate in proximity to each other to accomplish the joint force commander's mission. These two forces assist and complement each other with mutual support so they can achieve an objective that otherwise might not be attainable. Historically, commanders have employed special operations forces in the advance phases of operations. During extended or large-scale operations involving both conventional land and special operations forces, control measures take on added significance. These operations require the integration and synchronization of conventional and special operations missions. The tactical commander must consider capabilities and limitations of both conventional land and special operations forces, particularly in the areas of tactical mission command and sustainment. Exchanging liaison elements between the staffs of appropriate conventional and special operations forces further enhances integration of all forces concerned.

3-36. Improved access to joint capabilities gives commanders additional means to achieve mutual support. Those capabilities can extend the operating distances between Army units. Army commanders can substitute joint capabilities for mutual support between subordinate forces. Doing this multiplies supporting distance many times over. Army forces can then extend operations over greater areas at a higher tempo. Joint capabilities are especially useful when subordinate units operate in noncontiguous areas of operations that place units beyond a supporting range or supporting distance. However, depending on joint capabilities outside an Army commander's direct control entails accepting risk.

Chapter 4

Operational Art

This chapter defines operational art. It then discusses the application of operational art. Lastly it discusses the elements of operational art. It details how commanders and staffs apply these elements to understand, visualize, and describe to establish conditions to achieve a desired end state.

THE APPLICATION OF OPERATIONAL ART

4-1. *Operational art* is the cognitive approach by commanders and staffs—supported by their skill, knowledge, experience, creativity, and judgment—to develop strategies, campaigns, and operations to organize and employ military forces by integrating ends, ways, and means (JP 3-0). For Army forces, operational art is the pursuit of strategic objectives, in whole or in part, through the arrangement of tactical actions in time, space, and purpose. This approach enables commanders and staffs to use skill, knowledge, experience, and judgment to overcome the ambiguity and intricacies of a complex, ever changing, and uncertain operational environment to better understand the problem or problems at hand. Operational art applies to all aspects of operations and integrates ends, ways, and means, while accounting for risk. Operational art is applicable at all levels of war, not just to the operational level of war.

4-2. Army commanders focus on planning and executing operations and activities to achieve military objectives in support of the joint force commander's campaign plan. They use operational art and the principles of joint operations to envision how to establish conditions that accomplish their missions and achieve assigned objectives. Actions and interactions across the levels of war influence these conditions.

4-3. The twelve principles of joint operations represent important factors that affect the conduct of operations across the levels of war. (See figure 4-1 on page 4-2.) The principles are not a checklist. While commanders consider the principles in all operations, they do not apply in the same way to every situation. Rather, they summarize characteristics of successful operations. Their greatest value lies in educating the military professional. Applied to the study of past operations, the principles are powerful tools that can assist commanders in analyzing pending operations. While considering the principles, commanders synchronize efforts and determine if or when to deviate from the principles based on the current situation.

4-4. Through operational art and the principles of joint operations, commanders thoroughly analyze an operational environment. They determine the most effective and efficient methods for applying decisive action in various locations across multiple echelons.

4-5. When applying operational art, commanders and staff must create a shared understanding of purpose. This begins with open, continuous collaboration and dialogue between commanders at various echelons of command. Such collaboration and dialogue enables commanders to share an understanding of the problem and conditions of an operational environment. Effective collaboration facilitates assessment, fosters critical analysis, and anticipates opportunities and risk.

4-6. Operational art spans a continuum—from comprehensive strategic direction to concrete tactical actions. Bridging this continuum requires creative vision coupled with broad experience and knowledge. Without operational art, tactical actions devolve into a series of disconnected engagements that do not accomplish the mission or objectives of the joint force. Through operational art, commanders translate their operational approach into a concept of operations and ultimately into tactical tasks. Commanders then array forces and maneuver them to achieve a desired end state.

- **Objective**: Direct every military operation toward a clearly defined, decisive, and achievable goal.
- **Offensive**: Seize, retain, and exploit the initiative.
- **Mass**: Concentrate the effects of combat power at the most advantageous place and time to produce decisive results.
- **Maneuver**: Place the enemy in a position of disadvantage through the flexible application of combat power.
- **Economy of force**: Expend minimum essential combat power on secondary efforts in order to allocate the maximum possible combat power on primary efforts.
- **Unity of command**: Ensure unity of effort under one responsible commander for every objective.
- **Security**: Prevent the enemy from acquiring unexpected advantage.
- **Surprise**: Strike at a time or place or in a manner for which the enemy is unprepared.
- **Simplicity**: Increase the probability that plans and operations will be executed as intended by preparing clear, uncomplicated plans and concise orders.
- **Restraint**: Limit collateral damage and prevent the unnecessary use of force.
- **Perseverance**: Ensure the commitment necessary to attain the national strategic end state.
- **Legitimacy**: Maintain legal and moral authority in the conduct of operations.

(JP 3-0)

Figure 4-1. Principles of joint operations

4-7. Army design methodology assists commanders in developing their operational approach. Applying operational art requires a shared understanding of an operational environment with the problem analyzed through the Army design methodology. This understanding enables commanders to develop an operational approach to guide the force in establishing those conditions for lasting success. (See figure 4-2.) The *operational approach* is a description of the broad actions the force must take to transform current conditions into those desired at end state (JP 5-0). Commanders use a common doctrinal language to visualize and describe their operational approach. The operational approach provides a framework that relates tactical tasks to the desired end state. It provides a unifying purpose and focus to all operations.

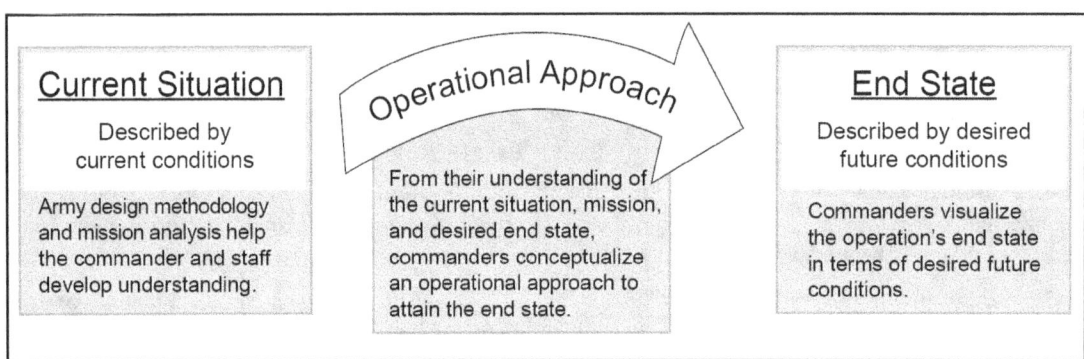

Figure 4-2. Operational approach

THE ELEMENTS OF OPERATIONAL ART

4-8. In applying operational art, commanders and their staffs use intellectual tools to help them understand an operational environment as well as visualize and describe their approach for conducting the operation. Collectively, this set of tools is known as the elements of operational art. These tools help commanders understand, visualize, and describe the integration and synchronization of the elements of combat power as well as their commander's intent and guidance. Commanders selectively use these tools in any operation. However, the tools' broadest application applies to long-term operations.

4-9. Within operational art, joint force commanders and staffs consider elements of operational design. Elements of operational design are individual tools that help the joint force commander and staff visualize and describe the broad operational approach. (See figure 4-3. See JP 3-0 for a discussion of the elements of operational design.) Army forces use elements of operational design when functioning as a joint force headquarters.

• Termination	• Direct and indirect approach
• Military end state	• Anticipation
• Objective	• Operational reach
• Effects	• Culmination
• Center of gravity	• Arranging operations
• Decisive point	• Force and functions
• Lines of operations and lines of effort	

Figure 4-3. Elements of operational design

4-10. As some elements of operational design apply only to joint force commanders, the Army modifies the elements of operational design into elements of operational art, adding Army specific elements. During the planning and execution of Army operations, Army commanders and staffs consider the elements of operational art as they assess the situation. (See figure 4-4.) They adjust current and future operations and plans as the operation unfolds, and reframe as necessary.

• End state and conditions	• Basing
• Center of gravity*	• Tempo
• Decisive points*	• Phasing and transitions
• Lines of operations and lines of effort*	• Culmination*
• Operational reach*	• Risk
*Common to elements of operational design	

Figure 4-4. Elements of operational art

END STATE AND CONDITIONS

4-11. The end state is a set of desired future conditions the commander wants to exist when an operation ends. Commanders include the end state in their planning guidance. A clearly defined end state promotes unity of effort; facilitates integration, synchronization, and disciplined initiative; and helps mitigate risk.

4-12. Army operations typically focus on attaining the military end state that may include contributions to establishing nonmilitary conditions. Commanders explicitly describe the end state and its conditions for every operation. Otherwise, missions become vague, and operations lose focus. Successful commanders direct every operation toward a clearly defined, conclusive, and attainable end state (goal).

4-13. The end state may evolve as an operation progresses. Commanders continuously monitor operations and evaluate their progress. Commanders use formal and informal assessment methods to assess their progress in achieving the end state and determine whether they need to reframe. The end state should anticipate future operations and set conditions for transitions. The end state should help commanders think through the conduct of operations to best facilitate transitions.

CENTERS OF GRAVITY

4-14. A *center of gravity* is the source of power that provides moral or physical strength, freedom of action, or will to act (JP 5-0). This definition states in modern terms the classic description offered by Clausewitz: "the hub of all power and movement, on which everything depends."[1] The loss of a center of

---

[1] © 1984. Reproduced with permission of Princeton University Press.

gravity can ultimately result in defeat. The center of gravity is a vital analytical tool for planning operations. It provides a focal point, identifying sources of strength and weakness.

4-15. Centers of gravity are not limited to military forces and can be either physical or moral. They are part of a dynamic perspective of an operational environment. Physical centers of gravity, such as a capital city or military force, are typically easier to identify, assess, and target. They can often be influenced solely by military means. In contrast, moral centers of gravity are intangible and more difficult to influence. They can include a charismatic leader, powerful ruling elite, religious tradition, tribal influence, or strong-willed populace. Military means alone usually prove ineffective when targeting moral centers of gravity. Affecting them requires the collective, integrated efforts of all instruments of national power.

4-16. Commanders analyze a center of gravity thoroughly and in detail. Faulty conclusions drawn from hasty or abbreviated analyses can adversely affect operations, waste critical resources, and incur undue risk. Thoroughly understanding an operational environment helps commanders identify and target enemy centers of gravity. This understanding encompasses how enemies organize, fight, and make decisions. It also includes their physical and moral strengths and weaknesses. In addition, commanders should understand how military forces interact with other government and civilian organizations. This understanding helps planners identify centers of gravity, their associated decisive points, and the best approach for achieving the desired end state.

DECISIVE POINTS

4-17. A *decisive point* is a geographic place, specific key event, critical factor, or function that, when acted upon, allows commanders to gain a marked advantage over an adversary or contribute materially to achieving success (JP 5-0). Decisive points help commanders select clear, conclusive, attainable objectives that directly contribute to achieving the end state. Geographic decisive points can include port facilities, distribution networks and nodes, and bases of operation. Specific events and elements of an enemy force may also be decisive points. Examples of such events include commitment of the enemy operational reserve and reopening a major oil refinery.

4-18. A common characteristic of decisive points is their importance to a center of gravity. A decisive point's importance requires the enemy to commit significant resources to defend it. The loss of a decisive point weakens a center of gravity and may expose more decisive points, eventually leading to an attack on the center of gravity itself. Decisive points are not centers of gravity; they are key to attacking or protecting centers of gravity. Commanders identify the decisive points that offer the greatest physical, temporal, or psychological advantage against centers of gravity.

4-19. Decisive points apply at both the operational and tactical levels shaping the design of operations. Combined arms maneuver and wide area security often focuses on achieving a position of physical, temporal, or psychological advantage with respect to one or more decisive points. Decisive points enable commanders to seize, retain, or exploit the initiative. Controlling them is essential to mission accomplishment. Enemy control of a decisive point may exhaust friendly momentum, force early culmination, or allow an enemy counterattack.

LINES OF OPERATIONS AND LINES OF EFFORT

4-20. Lines of operations and lines of effort link objectives to the end state. Commanders may describe an operation along lines of operations, lines of effort, or a combination of both. The combination of them may change based on the conditions within the area of operations. Commanders synchronize and sequence actions, deliberately creating complementary and reinforcing effects. The lines then converge on the well-defined, commonly understood end state outlined in the commander's intent.

4-21. Commanders at all levels may use lines of operations and lines of effort to develop tasks and allocate resources. Commanders may designate one line as the decisive operation and others as shaping operations. Commanders synchronize and sequence related actions along multiple lines. Seeing these relationships helps commanders assess progress toward achieving the end state as forces perform tasks and accomplish missions.

Lines of Operations

4-22. A *line of operations* **is a line that defines the directional orientation of a force in time and space in relation to the enemy and that links the force with its base of operations and objectives.** Lines of operations connect a series of decisive points that lead to control of a geographic or force-oriented objective. Operations designed using lines of operations generally consist of a series of actions executed according to a well-defined sequence. **A force operates on *interior lines* when its operations diverge from a central point. A force operates on *exterior lines* when its operations converge on the enemy.** Combined arms maneuver is often designed using lines of operations. These lines tie offensive and defensive tasks to the geographic and positional references in the area of operations.

Lines of Effort

4-23. A *line of effort* **is a line that links multiple tasks using the logic of purpose rather than geographical reference to focus efforts toward establishing operational and strategic conditions.** Lines of effort are essential to long-term planning when positional references to an enemy or adversary have little relevance. In operations involving many nonmilitary factors, lines of effort may be the only way to link tasks to the end state. Lines of effort are often essential to helping commanders visualize how military capabilities can support the other instruments of national power.

4-24. Commanders use lines of effort to describe how they envision their operations creating the intangible end state conditions. These lines of effort show how individual actions relate to each other and to achieving the end state. Commanders often visualize wide area security using stability and defense support of civil authorities tasks along lines of effort. These tasks link military actions with the broader interagency effort across the levels of war. As operations progress, commanders may modify the lines of effort after assessing conditions and collaborating with multinational military and civilian partners.

Combining Lines of Operations and Lines of Effort

4-25. Commanders use lines of operations and lines of effort to connect objectives to a central, unifying purpose. The difference between lines of operations and lines of effort is that lines of operations are oriented on physical linkages while lines of effort are oriented on logical linkages. Combining lines of operations and lines of effort allows a commander to include stability or defense support of civil authorities tasks in the long-term plan. This combination helps commanders incorporate these tasks that support wide area security, setting the end state conditions for transitions in the operation.

OPERATIONAL REACH

4-26. *Operational reach* is the distance and duration across which a joint force can successfully employ military capabilities (JP 3-0). It reflects the ability to achieve success through a well-conceived operational approach. Operational reach is a tether; it is a function of intelligence, protection, sustainment, endurance, and relative combat power. The limit of a unit's operational reach is its culminating point. It equalizes the natural tension between endurance, momentum, and protection.

4-27. Endurance refers to the ability to employ combat power anywhere for protracted periods. It stems from the ability to create, protect, and sustain a force, regardless of the distance from its base and the austerity of the environment. Endurance involves anticipating requirements and making the most effective, efficient use of available resources. Their endurance gives Army forces their campaign quality. It makes permanent the transitory effects of other capabilities.

4-28. Momentum comes from seizing the initiative and executing high-tempo operations that overwhelm enemy resistance. It is the temporal advantage derived from combined arms maneuver. Commanders control momentum by maintaining focus and pressure. They set a tempo that prevents exhaustion and maintains sustainment. A sustainable tempo extends operational reach. Commanders maintain momentum by anticipating and transitioning rapidly between any combination of offensive, defensive, stability, or defense support of civil authorities tasks. Sometimes commanders push the force to its culminating point to take maximum advantage of an opportunity. For example, exploitations and pursuits often involve pushing all available forces to the limit of their endurance to capitalize on momentum and retain the initiative.

4-29. Protection is an important contributor to operational reach. Commanders anticipate how enemy actions and environmental factors might disrupt operations and then determine the protection capabilities required to maintain sufficient reach. Protection closely relates to endurance and momentum. It also contributes to the commander's ability to extend operations in time and space. The protection warfighting function helps commanders maintain the force's integrity and combat power.

4-30. Commanders and staffs consider operational reach to ensure Army forces accomplish their missions before culminating. Commanders continually strive to extend operational reach. They assess friendly and enemy force status and civil considerations, anticipate culmination, and plan operational pauses if necessary. Commanders have studied and reflected on the challenge of conducting and sustaining operations over long distances and times. History contains many examples of operations hampered by inadequate operational reach. Achieving the desired end state requires forces with the operational reach to establish and maintain wide area security so they can successfully transition to the end state conditions.

BASING

4-31. Army basing overseas typically falls into two general categories: permanent (bases or installations) and nonpermanent (base camps). A *base* is a locality from which operations are projected or supported (JP 4-0). Generally, bases are in host nations where the United States has a long-term lease agreement and a status-of-forces agreement. A base camp is an evolving military facility that supports the military operations of a deployed unit and provides the necessary support and services for sustained operations. They are nonpermanent by design and designated as a base when the intention is to make them permanent. Bases or base camps may have a specific purpose (such as serving as an intermediate staging base, a logistics base, or a base camp) or they may be multifunctional. The longer base camps exist, the more they exhibit many of the same characteristics in terms of the support and services provided and types of facilities developed. A base or base camp has a defined perimeter and established access controls and takes advantage of natural and man-made features.

4-32. Basing may be joint or single Service and will routinely support both U.S. and multinational forces, as well as interagency partners, operating anywhere along the range of military operations. Commanders often designate a specific area as a base or base camp and assign responsibility to a single commander for protection and terrain management within the base. Units located within the base or base camp are under the tactical control of the base or base camp commander for base security and defense. Within large echelon support areas, controlling commanders may designate base clusters for mutual protection and mission command.

4-33. When a base camp expands to include clusters of sustainment, headquarters, and other supporting units, commanders may designate a support area. Echelon commanders designate a support area. This specific surface area facilitates the positioning, employment, and protection of resources required to sustain, enable, and control tactical operations. Within a support area, a designated unit such as a brigade combat team or maneuver enhancement brigade provides area security, terrain management, movement control, mobility support, clearance of fires, and required tactical combat forces. Area security operations focus on the protected force, base or base camp, route, or area. This allows sustainment units to focus on their primary function.

4-34. Army forces typically rely on a mix of bases and base camps to serve as intermediate staging bases, lodgments (subsequently developed into base camps or potentially bases), and forward operating bases. These bases and base camps deploy and employ land power simultaneously to operational depth. They establish and maintain strategic reach for deploying forces and ensure sufficient operational reach to extend operations in time and space.

4-35. An *intermediate staging base* is a tailorable, temporary location used for staging forces, sustainment and/or extraction into and out of an operational area (JP 3-35). At the intermediate staging base, units are unloaded from intertheater lift, reassembled and integrated with their equipment, and then moved by intratheater lift into the area of operations. The theater army commander provides extensive support to Army forces transiting the base. The combatant commander may designate the theater army commander to command the base or provide a headquarters suitable for the task. Intermediate staging bases are established near, but normally not in, the joint operations area. They often are located in the supported combatant commander's area of responsibility. For land forces, intermediate staging bases may be located in the area of operations. However, they are always established outside the range of enemy fires and beyond the enemy's political sphere of influence.

4-36. A *lodgment* is a designated area in a hostile or potentially hostile operational area that, when seized and held, makes the continuous landing of troops and materiel possible and provides maneuver space for subsequent operations (JP 3-18). Identifying and preparing the initial lodgment significantly influences the conduct of an operation. Lodgments should expand to allow easy access to strategic sealift and airlift, offer adequate space for storage, facilitate transshipment of supplies and equipment, and be accessible to multiple lines of communications. Typically, deploying forces establish lodgments near key points of entry in the operational area that offers central access to air, land, and sea transportation hubs.

4-37. Forward operating bases may be used for an extended time and are often critical to wide area security. During protracted operations, they may be expanded and improved to establish a more permanent presence. The scale and complexity of the forward operating bases, however, directly relates to the size of the force required to maintain it. A large forward operating base with extensive facilities requires a much larger security force than a smaller, austere base. Commanders weigh whether to expand and improve forward operating bases against the type and number of forces available to secure it, the expected length of the forward deployment, and the force's sustainment requirements.

TEMPO

4-38. *Tempo* **is the relative speed and rhythm of military operations over time with respect to the enemy**. It reflects the rate of military action. Controlling tempo helps commanders keep the initiative during combat operations or rapidly establish a sense of normalcy during humanitarian crises. During operations dominated by combined arms maneuver, commanders normally seek to maintain a higher tempo than the enemy does; a rapid tempo can overwhelm an enemy's ability to counter friendly actions. It is the key to achieving a temporal advantage during combined arms maneuver. During operations dominated by wide area security, commanders act quickly to control events and deny the enemy positions of advantage. By acting faster than the situation deteriorates, commanders can change the dynamics of a crisis and restore stability.

4-39. Commanders control tempo throughout the conduct of operations. First, they formulate operations that stress the complementary and reinforcing effects of simultaneous and sequential operations. They synchronize those operations in time and space to degrade enemy capabilities throughout the area of operations. Second, commanders avoid unnecessary engagements. This practice includes bypassing resistance at times and places commanders do not consider decisive. Third, through mission command they enable subordinates to exercise initiative and act independently. Controlling tempo requires both audacity and patience. Audacity initiates the actions needed to develop a situation; patience allows a situation to develop until the force can strike at the most crucial time and place. Ultimately, the goal is maintaining a tempo appropriate to retaining the initiative and achieving the end state.

4-40. Army forces expend more energy and resources when operating at a high tempo. Commanders assess the force's capacity to operate at a higher tempo based on its performance and available resources. An effective operational design varies tempo throughout an operation to increase endurance while maintaining appropriate speed and momentum. There is more to tempo than speed. While speed can be important, commanders mitigate speed with endurance.

PHASING AND TRANSITIONS

4-41. **A *phase* is a planning and execution tool used to divide an operation in duration or activity**. A change in phase usually involves a change of mission, task organization, or rules of engagement. Phasing helps in planning and controlling and may be indicated by time, distance, terrain, or an event. The ability of Army forces to extend operations in time and space, coupled with a desire to dictate tempo, often presents commanders with more objectives and decisive points than the force can engage simultaneously. This may require commanders and staffs to consider sequencing operations.

4-42. Phasing is critical to arranging all tasks of an operation that cannot be conducted simultaneously. It describes how the commander envisions the overall operation unfolding. It is the logical expression of the commander's visualization in time. Within a phase, a large portion of the force executes similar or mutually supporting activities. Achieving a specified condition or set of conditions typically marks the end of a phase.

4-43. Simultaneity, depth, and tempo are vital to all operations. However, they cannot always be attained to the degree desired. In such cases, commanders limit the number of objectives and decisive points engaged simultaneously. They deliberately sequence certain actions to maintain tempo while focusing combat power at a decisive point in time and space. Commanders combine simultaneous and sequential tasks of an operation to establish the end state conditions.

4-44. Phasing can extend operational reach. Only when the force lacks the capability to accomplish the mission in a single action do commanders phase the operation. Each phase should strive to—
- Focus effort.
- Concentrate combat power in time and space at a decisive point.
- Accomplish its objectives deliberately and logically.

4-45. Transitions mark a change of focus between phases or between the ongoing operation and execution of a branch or sequel. Shifting priorities between the core competencies or among offensive, defensive, stability, and defense support of civil authorities tasks also involve a transition. Transitions require planning and preparation well before their execution to maintain the momentum and tempo of operations. The force is vulnerable during transitions, and commanders establish clear conditions for their execution.

4-46. A transition occurs for several reasons. It may occur from an operation dominated by combined arms maneuver to one dominated by wide area security. Transitions also occur with the delivery of essential services or retention of infrastructure needed for reconstruction. An unexpected change in conditions may require commanders to direct an abrupt transition between phases. In such cases, the overall composition of the force remains unchanged despite sudden changes in mission, task organization, and rules of engagement. Typically, task organization evolves to meet changing conditions; however, transition planning must also account for changes in mission. Commanders continuously assess the situation and task-organize and cycle their forces to retain the initiative. They strive to achieve changes in emphasis without incurring an operational pause.

4-47. Commanders identify potential transitions during planning and account for them throughout execution. Considerations for identifying potential transitions should include—
- Forecasting in advance when and how to transition.
- Arranging tasks to facilitate transitions.
- Creating a task organization that anticipates transitions.
- Rehearsing certain transitions such as from defense to counterattack or offense to defense support of civil authorities and restoration of essential services.
- Ensuring the force understands different rules of engagement during transitions.

4-48. Commanders should appreciate the time required to both plan for and execute transitions. Assessment ensures that commanders measure progress toward such transitions and take appropriate actions to prepare for and execute them.

CULMINATION

4-49. **The *culminating point* is that point in time and space at which a force no longer possesses the capability to continue its current form of operations.** Culmination represents a crucial shift in relative combat power. It is relevant to both attackers and defenders at each level of war. While conducting offensive tasks, the culminating point occurs when the force cannot continue the attack and must assume a defensive posture or execute an operational pause. While conducting defensive tasks, it occurs when the force can no longer defend itself and must withdraw or risk destruction. The culminating point is more difficult to identify when Army forces conduct stability tasks. Two conditions can result in culmination: units being too dispersed to achieve wide area security and units lacking required resources to achieve the end state. While conducting defense support of civil authorities tasks, culmination may occur if forces must respond to more catastrophic events than they can manage simultaneously. That situation results in culmination due to exhaustion.

4-50. Culmination may be a planned event. In such cases, the concept of operations predicts which part of the force will culminate, and the task organization includes additional forces to assume the mission. Typically culmination is caused by direct combat actions or higher echelon resourcing decisions. It relates to the force's ability to generate and apply combat power and is not a lasting condition. To continue operations, commanders may reinforce or reconstitute tactical units.

RISK

4-51. Risk, uncertainty, and chance are inherent in all military operations. When commanders accept risk, they create opportunities to seize, retain, and exploit the initiative and achieve decisive results. The willingness to incur risk is often the key to exposing enemy weaknesses that the enemy considers beyond friendly reach. Understanding risk requires assessments coupled with boldness and imagination. Successful commanders assess and mitigate risk continuously throughout the operations process.

4-52. Inadequate planning and preparation recklessly risks forces. It is equally rash to delay action while waiting for perfect intelligence and synchronization. Reasonably estimating and intentionally accepting risk is fundamental to conducting operations and essential to mission command. Experienced commanders balance audacity and imagination with risk and uncertainty to strike at a time and place and in a manner wholly unexpected by enemy forces. This is the essence of surprise. It results from carefully considering and accepting risk.

4-53. Commanders accept risk and seek opportunity to create and maintain the conditions necessary to seize, retain, and exploit the initiative and achieve decisive results. During execution, opportunity is fleeting. The surest means to create opportunity is to accept risk while minimizing hazards to friendly forces. A good operational approach considers risk and uncertainty equally with friction and chance. The final plans and orders then provide the flexibility commanders need to take advantage of opportunity in a highly competitive and dynamic environment.

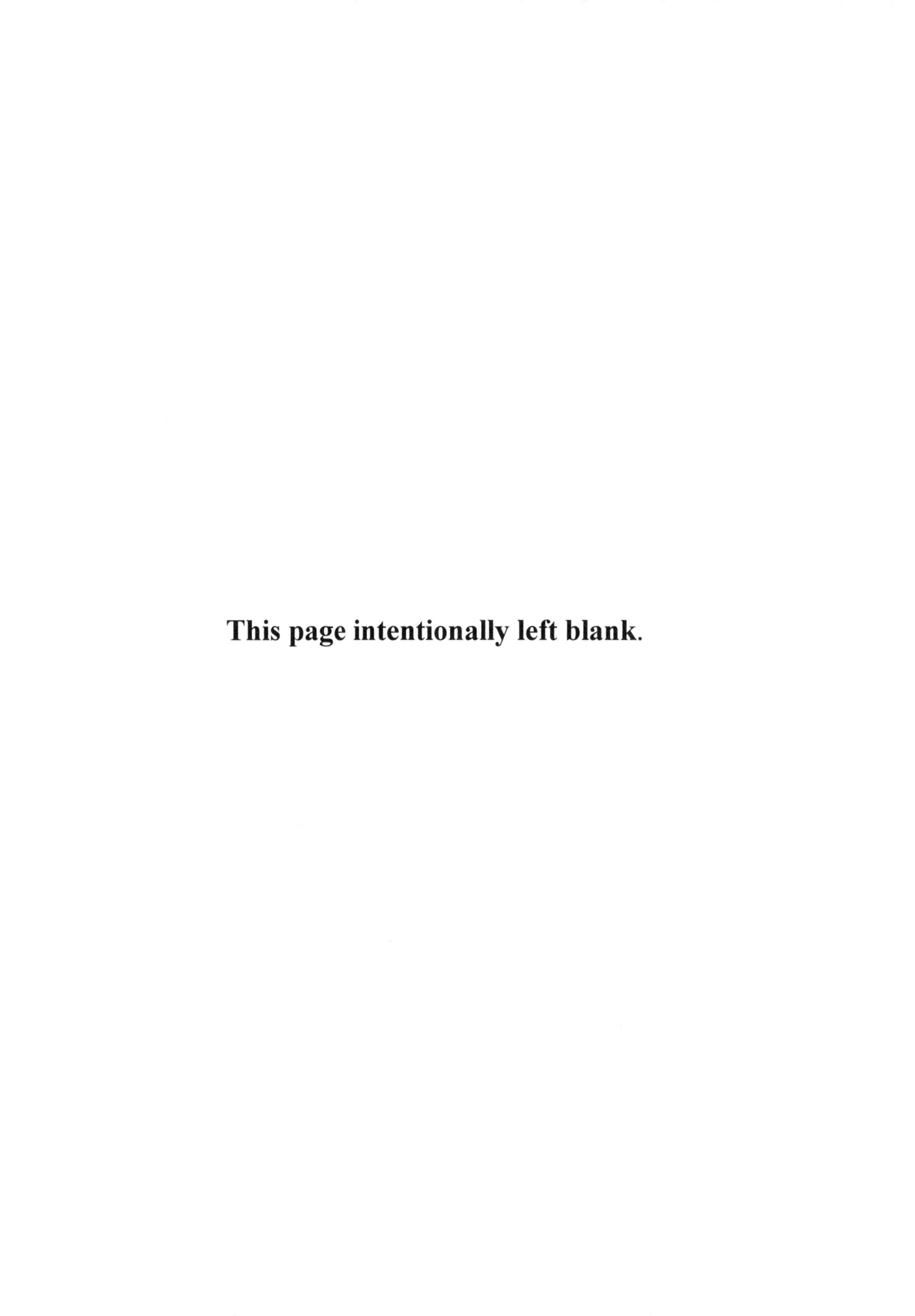

This page intentionally left blank.

Source Notes

These are the sources used for historical examples that are cited and quoted in this publication. They are listed by page number.

v   FM 3-0, Change 1, *Operations*, (Washington, DC: Department of Defense, 22 February 2011).

4-3   Clausewitz, Carl von, *On War*, edited by Michael Howard and Peter Paret (Princeton: Princeton University Press, 1984), 595-596.

This page intentionally left blank.

Glossary

The glossary lists acronyms and terms with Army or joint definitions. Where Army and joint definitions differ, (Army) precedes the definition. Terms for which ADRP 3-0 is the proponent are marked with an asterisk (*). The proponent manual for other terms is listed in parentheses after the definition.

SECTION I – ACRONYMS AND ABBREVIATIONS

ADP	Army doctrine publication
ADRP	Army doctrine reference publication
AR	Army regulation
ARFOR	Army forces
DA	Department of the Army
DOD	Department of Defense
FM	field manual
JP	joint publication
METT-TC	mission, enemy, terrain and weather, troops and support available, time available, civil considerations
PMESII-PT	political, military, economic, social, information, infrastructure, physical environment, time
U.S.	United States

SECTION II – TERMS

adversary

A party acknowledged as potentially hostile to a friendly party and against which the use of force may be envisaged. (JP 3-0)

alliance

The relationship that results from a formal agreement between two or more nations for broad, long-term objectives that further the common interests of the members. (JP 3-0)

area of influence

A geographical area wherein a commander is directly capable of influencing operations by maneuver or fire support systems normally under the commander's command or control. (JP 3-0)

area of interest

That area of concern to the commander, including the area of influence, areas adjacent thereto, and extending into enemy territory. This area also includes areas occupied by enemy forces who could jeopardize the accomplishment of the mission. (JP 3-0)

area of operations

An operational area defined by the joint force commander for land and maritime forces that should be large enough to accomplish their missions and protect their forces. (JP 3-0)

assessment

Determination of the progress toward accomplishing a task, creating a condition, or achieving an objective. (JP 3-0)

base

A locality from which operations are projected or supported. (JP 4-0)

campaign

A series of related major operations aimed at achieving strategic and operational objectives within a given time and space. (JP 5-0)

center of gravity

The source of power that provides moral or physical strength, freedom of action, or will to act. (JP 5-0)

*close area

In contiguous areas of operations, an area assigned to a maneuver force that extends from its subordinates' rear boundaries to its own forward boundary.

*close combat

Warfare carried out on land in a direct-fire fight, supported by direct and indirect fires and other assets.

coalition

An arrangement between two or more nations for common action. (JP 5-0)

*combat power

(Army) The total means of destructive, constructive, and information capabilities that a military unit or formation can apply at a given time.

*combined arms

The synchronized and simultaneous application of arms to achieve an effect greater than if each arm was used separately or sequentially.

combined arms maneuver

The application of the elements of combat power in unified action to defeat enemy ground forces; to seize, occupy, and defend land areas; and to achieve physical, temporal, and psychological advantages over the enemy to seize and exploit the initiative. (ADP 3-0)

command

The authority that a commander in the armed forces lawfully exercises over subordinates by virtue of rank or assignment. Command includes the authority and responsibility for effectively using available resources and for planning the employment of, organizing, directing, coordinating, and controlling military forces for the accomplishment of assigned missions. It also includes responsibility for health, welfare, morale, and discipline of assigned personnel. (JP 1)

commander's intent

A clear and concise expression of the purpose of the operation and the desired military end state that supports mission command, provides focus to the staff, and helps subordinate and supporting commanders act to achieve the commander's desired results without further orders, even when the operation does not unfold as planned. (JP 3-0)

*culminating point

(Army) That point in time and space at which a force no longer possesses the capability to continue its current form of operations.

*cyber electromagnetic activities

Activities leveraged to seize, retain, and exploit an advantage over adversaries and enemies in both cyberspace and the electromagnetic spectrum, while simultaneously denying and degrading adversary and enemy use of the same and protecting the mission command system.

*decisive action

The continuous, simultaneous combinations of offensive, defensive, and stability or defense support of civil authorities tasks.

*decisive operation

The operation that directly accomplishes the mission.

decisive point

A geographic place, specific key event, critical factor, or function that, when acted upon, allows commanders to gain a marked advantage over an adversary or contribute materially to achieving success. (JP 5-0)

*deep area

In contiguous areas of operations, an area forward of the close area that a commander uses to shape enemy forces before they are encountered or engaged in the close area.

*defeat mechanism

The method through which friendly forces accomplish their mission against enemy opposition.

*defensive task

A task conducted to defeat an enemy attack, gain time, economize forces, and develop conditions favorable for offensive or stability tasks.

*enemy

A party identified as hostile against which the use of force is authorized.

*exterior lines

Lines on which a force operates when its operations converge on the enemy.

*fires warfighting function

The related tasks and systems that provide collective and coordinated use of Army indirect fires, air and missile defense, and joint fires through the targeting process.

*force tailoring

The process of determining the right mix of forces and the sequence of their deployment in support of a joint force commander.

homeland defense

The protection of United States sovereignty, territory, domestic population, and critical defense infrastructure against external threats and aggression or other threats as directed by the President. (JP 3-27)

*hybrid threat

The diverse and dynamic combination of regular forces, irregular forces, terrorist forces, and/or criminal elements unified to achieve mutually benefitting effects.

*individual initiative

The willingness to act in the absence of orders, when existing orders no longer fit the situation, or when unforeseen opportunities or threats arise.

*inform and influence activities

The integration of designated information-related capabilities in order to synchronize themes, messages, and actions with operations to inform United States and global audiences, influence foreign audiences, and affect adversary and enemy decisionmaking.

information collection

An activity that synchronizes and integrates the planning and employment of sensors and assets as well as the processing, exploitation, and dissemination systems in direct support of current and future operations. (FM 3-55)

*intelligence warfighting function

The related tasks and systems that facilitate understanding the enemy, terrain, and civil considerations.

interagency coordination

Within the context of Department of Defense involvement, the coordination that occurs between elements of Department of Defense, and engaged US Government agencies and departments for the purpose of achieving an objective. (JP 3-0)

intergovernmental organization

An organization created by a formal agreement between two or more governments on a global, regional, or functional basis to protect and promote national interests shared by member states. (JP 3-08)

*interior lines

Lines on which a force operates when its operations diverge from a central point.

intermediate staging base

A tailorable, temporary location used for staging forces, sustainment and/or extraction into and out of an operational area. (JP 3-35)

interorganizational coordination

The interaction that occurs among elements of the Department of Defense; engaged United States Government agencies; state, territorial, local, and tribal agencies; foreign military forces and government agencies; intergovernmental organizations; nongovernmental organizations; and the private sector. (JP 3-08)

*landpower

The ability—by threat, force, or occupation—to gain, sustain, and exploit control over land, resources, and people.

*line of effort

(Army) A line that links multiple tasks using the logic of purpose rather than geographical reference to focus efforts toward establishing operational and strategic conditions.

*line of operations

(Army) A line that defines the directional orientation of a force in time and space in relation to the enemy and that links the force with its base of operations and objectives.

lodgment

A designated area in a hostile or potentially hostile operational area that, when seized and held, makes the continuous landing of troops and materiel possible and provides maneuver space for subsequent operations. (JP 3-18)

*main effort

A designated subordinate unit whose mission at a given point in time is most critical to overall mission success.

major operation

A series of tactical actions (battles, engagements, strikes) conducted by combat forces of a single or several Services, coordinated in time and place, to achieve strategic or operational objectives in an operational area. (JP 3-0)

*mission command warfighting function

The related tasks and systems that develop and integrate those activities enabling a commander to balance the art of command and the science of control in order to integrate the other warfighting functions.

*movement and maneuver warfighting function

The related tasks and systems that move and employ forces to achieve a position of relative advantage over the enemy and other threats.

multinational operations

A collective term to describe military actions conducted by forces of two or more nations, usually undertaken within the structure of a coalition or alliance. (JP 3-16)

mutual support

That support which units render each other against an enemy, because of their assigned tasks, their position relative to each other and to the enemy, and their inherent capabilities. (JP 3-31)

*neutral

(Army) A party identified as neither supporting nor opposing friendly or enemy forces.

nongovernmental organization

A private, self-governing, not-for-profit organization dedicated to alleviating human suffering; and/or promoting education, health care, economic development, environmental protection, human rights, and conflict resolution; and/or encouraging the establishment of democratic institutions and civil society. (JP 3-08)

*offensive task

A task conducted to defeat and destroy enemy forces and seize terrain, resources, and population centers.

operational approach

A description of the broad actions the force must take to transform current conditions into those desired at end state. (JP 5-0)

operational art

The cognitive approach by commanders and staffs—supported by their skill, knowledge, experience, creativity, and judgment—to develop strategies, campaigns, and operations to organize and employ military forces by integrating ends, ways, and means. (JP 3-0)

operational environment

A composite of the conditions, circumstances, and influences that affect the employment of capabilities and bear on the decisions of the commander. (JP 3-0)

*operational initiative

Setting or dictating the terms of action throughout an operation.

operational reach

The distance and duration across which a joint force can successfully employ military capabilities. (JP 3-0)

other government agency

Within the context of interagency coordination, a non Department of Defense agency of the United States Government. (JP 1)

*phase

(Army) A planning and execution tool used to divide an operation in duration or activity.

*protection warfighting function

The related tasks and systems that preserve the force so the commander can apply maximum combat power to accomplish the mission

rules for the use of force

Directives issued to guide United States forces on the use of force during various operations. These directives may take the form of execute orders, deployment orders, memoranda of agreement, or plans. (JP 3-28)

rules of engagement

Directives issued by competent military authority that delineate the circumstances and limitations under which United States forces will initiate and/or continue combat engagement with other forces encountered. (JP 1-04)

security cooperation

All Department of Defense interactions with foreign defense establishments to build defense relationships that promote specific US security interests, develop allied and friendly military capabilities for self-defense and multinational operations, and provide US forces with peacetime and contingency access to a host nation. (JP 3-22)

*shaping operation

An operation that establishes conditions for the decisive operation through effects on the enemy, other actors, and the terrain.

*stability mechanism

The primary method through which friendly forces affect civilians in order to attain conditions that support establishing a lasting, stable peace.

*support area

In contiguous areas of operations, an area for any command that extends from its rear boundary forward to the rear boundary of the next lower level of command

*supporting distance

The distance between two units that can be traveled in time for one to come to the aid of the other and prevent its defeat by an enemy or ensure it regains control of a civil situation.

*supporting effort

A designated subordinate unit with a mission that supports the success of the main effort.

*supporting range

The distance one unit may be geographically separated from a second unit yet remain within the maximum range of the second unit's weapons systems.

*sustaining operation

An operation at any echelon that enables the decisive operation or shaping operation by generating and maintaining combat power.

*sustainment warfighting function

The related tasks and systems that provide support and services to ensure freedom of action, extend operational reach, and prolong endurance.

synchronization

The arrangement of military actions in time, space, and purpose to produce maximum relative combat power at a decisive place and time. (JP 2-0)

*task-organizing

The act of designing an operating force, support staff, or sustainment package of specific size and composition to meet a unique task or mission.

*tempo

The relative speed and rhythm of military operations over time with respect to the enemy.

*threat

Any combination of actors, entities, or forces that have the capability and intent to harm United States forces, United States national interests, or the homeland.

unified action

The the synchronization, coordination, and/or integration of the activities of governmental and nongovernmental entities with military operations to achieve unity of effort. (JP 1)

*unified action partners

Those military forces, governmental and nongovernmental organizations, and elements of the private sector with whom Army forces plan, coordinate, synchronize, and integrate during the conduct of operations.

unified land operations

How the Army seizes, retains, and exploits the initiative to gain and maintain a position of relative advantage in sustained land operations through simultaneous offensive, defensive, and stability operations in order to prevent or deter conflict, prevail in war, and create the conditions for favorable conflict resolution. (ADP 3-0)

*warfighting function

> A group of tasks and systems (people, organizations, information, and processes) united by a common purpose that commanders use to accomplish missions and training objectives.

wide area security

> The application of the elements of combat power in unified action to protect populations, forces, infrastructure, and activities; to deny the enemy positions of advantage; and to consolidate gains in order to retain the initiative. (ADP 3-0)

This page intentionally left blank.

References

Field manuals and selected joint publications are listed by new number followed by old number.

REQUIRED PUBLICATIONS

These documents must be available to intended users of this publication.

FM 1-02 (101-5-1). *Operational Terms and Graphics*. 21 September 2004.

JP 1-02. *Department of Defense Dictionary of Military and Associated Terms*. 8 November 2010.

RELATED PUBLICATIONS

These documents contain relevant supplemental information.

JOINT PUBLICATIONS

Most joint publications are available online: <http://www.dtic.mil/doctrine/new_pubs/jointpub.htm.>

JP 1. *Doctrine for the Armed Forces of the United States*. 02 May 2007.

JP 1-04. *Legal Support to Military Operations*. 17 August 2011.

JP 2-0. *Joint Intelligence*. 22 June 2007.

JP 3-0. *Joint Operations*. 11 August 2011.

JP 3-05. *Special Operations*. 18 April 2011.

JP 3-07.2. *Antiterrorism*. 24 November 2010.

JP 3-07.3. *Peace Operations*. 17 October 2007.

JP 3-08. *Interorganizational Coordination During Joint Operations*. 24 June 2011.

JP 3-16. *Multinational Operations*. 7 March 2007.

JP 3-18. *Joint Forcible Entry Operations*. 16 June 2008.

JP 3-22. *Foreign Internal Defense*. 12 July 2010.

JP 3-24. *Counterinsurgency Operations*. 5 October 2009.

JP 3-27. *Homeland Defense*. 12 July 2007.

JP 3-28. *Civil Support*. 14 September 2007.

JP 3-29. *Foreign Humanitarian Assistance*. 17 March 2009.

JP 3-31. *Command and Control for Joint Land Operations*. 29 June 2010.

JP 3-35. *Deployment and Redeployment Operations*. 7 May 2007.

JP 3-40. *Combating Weapons of Mass Destruction*. 10 June 2009.

JP 3-50. *Personnel Recovery*. 20 December 2011.

JP 3-57. *Civil-Military Operations*. 08 July 2008.

JP 3-68. *Noncombatant Evacuation Operations*. 23 December 2010.

JP 4-0. *Joint Logistics*. 18 July 2008.

JP 5-0. *Joint Operation Planning*. 11 August 2011.

ARMY PUBLICATIONS

Most Army doctrinal publications are available online: <http://www.apd.army.mil/>.

ADP 3-0 (FM 3-0). *Unified Land Operations*. 10 October 2011.

AR 12-1. *Security Assistance, Training, and Export Policy*. 23 July 2010.

AR 350-1. *Army Training and Leader Development*. 18 Decemeber 2009.

ATTP 4-02 (FM 4-02). *Army Health System*. 7 October 2011.

FM 1-0. *Human Resources Support.* 6 April 2010.

FM 2-0. *Intelligence.* 23 March 2010.

FM 3-05. *Army Special Operations Forces.* 1 December 2010.

FM 3-05.2 (FM 3-05.137 and FM 3-05.202). *Foreign Internal Defense.* 1 September 2011.

FM 3-07. *Stability Operations.* 6 October 2008.

FM 3-07.1. *Security Force Assistance.* 1 May 2009.

FM 3-16 (FM 100-8). *The Army in Multinational Operations.* 20 May 2010.

FM 3-24 (FMI 3-07.22). *Counterinsurgency.* 15 December 2006.

FM 3-28. *Civil Support Operations.* 20 August 2010.

FM 3-35 (FMI 3-35 and FM 4-01.011). *Army Deployment and Redeployment.* 21 April 2010.

FM 3-50.1. *Army Personnel Recovery.* 21 November 2011.

FM 3-55. *Information Collection.* 23 April 2012.

FM 3-90. *Tactics.* 4 July 2001.

FM 4-0. *Sustainment.* 30 April 2009.

FM 6-22 (FM 22-100). *Army Leadership.* 12 October 2006.

FM 27-10. *The Law of Land Warfare.* 18 July 1956.

REFERENCED FORMS

DA Form 2028. *Recommended Changes to Publications and Blank Forms.*

Index

Entries are by paragraph number.

Entries are by paragraph number.

Entries are by paragraph number.

This page intentionally left blank.

By order of the Secretary of the Army:

RAYMOND T. ODIERNO
General, United States Army
Chief of Staff

Official:

JOYCE E. MORROW
Administrative Assistant to the
Secretary of the Army
1211401

DISTRIBUTION:

Active Army, Army National Guard, and United States Army Reserve: To be distributed in accordance with the initial distribution number (IDN) 110502, requirements for ADRP 3-0.

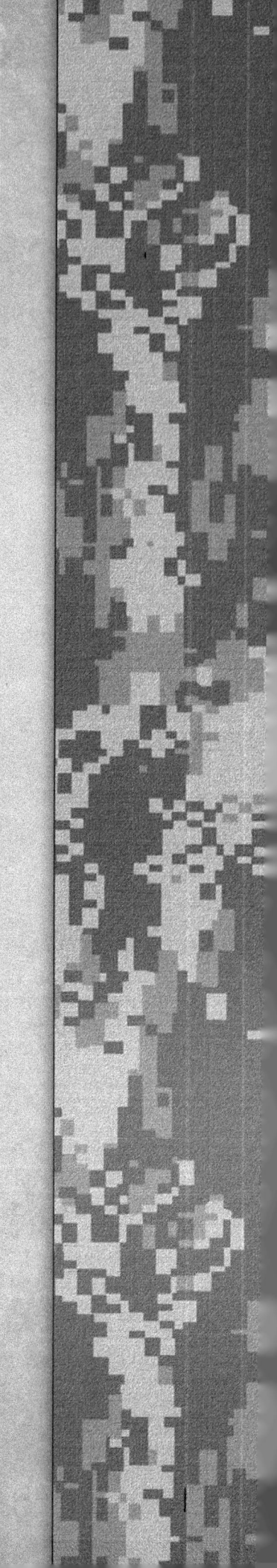

PIN: 102803-000

www.ingramcontent.com/pod-product-compliance
Lightning Source LLC
Chambersburg PA
CBHW080851010626

R18375900001B/R183759PG45790CBX00010B/19